Gandikota
CANYON
The Unseen Beauty

I0502957

KORUVOR

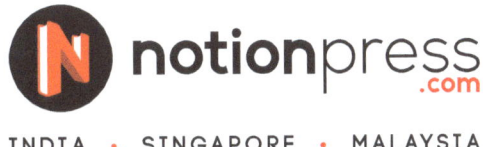

INDIA • SINGAPORE • MALAYSIA

Notion Press

Old No. 38, New No. 6
McNichols Road, Chetpet
Chennai - 600 031

First Published by Notion Press 2019
Copyright © Koruvor 2019
All Rights Reserved.

ISBN 978-1-64546-480-8

Dedicated to my parents

Acknowledgments

Thankful to so many.

Thanks to the person who worked so hard in such a short period of time—Bina Nayak of binanayak.com—who put in all the work to help in compiling this and making the illustrations.

The people of Gandikota Fort, who live in and around Gandikota, for welcoming tons of visitors.

Mr. Tavaa Obul Reddy (Author of *A Guide To Gandikoat Fort*) for his knowledge of the fort.
Mr. Majid, the cab operator, for assisting and planning the trip.
The Notion Press team.

Thanks to my family, especially my mother, father, my grandparents and love for books. Thanks to my brothers and my sisters-in-law, my sister and brother-in-law, and the rest of my family from my uncles in Texas and Georgia to my aunt and cousins in Paris, Kansas, Missouri and Texas, who share a common love for books, for their encouragement.

Thanks to my assistants and cooks.

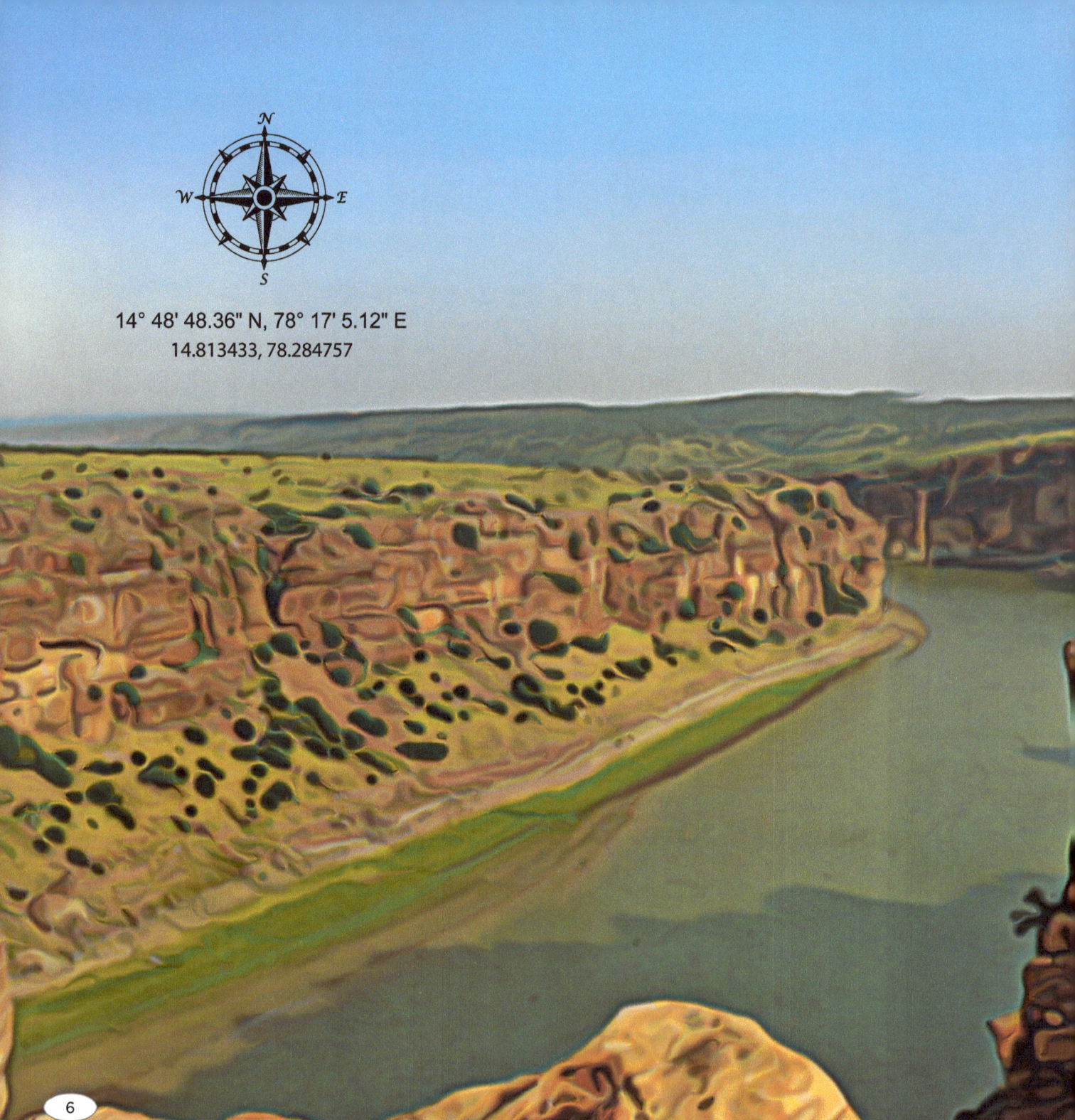

14° 48' 48.36" N, 78° 17' 5.12" E
14.813433, 78.284757

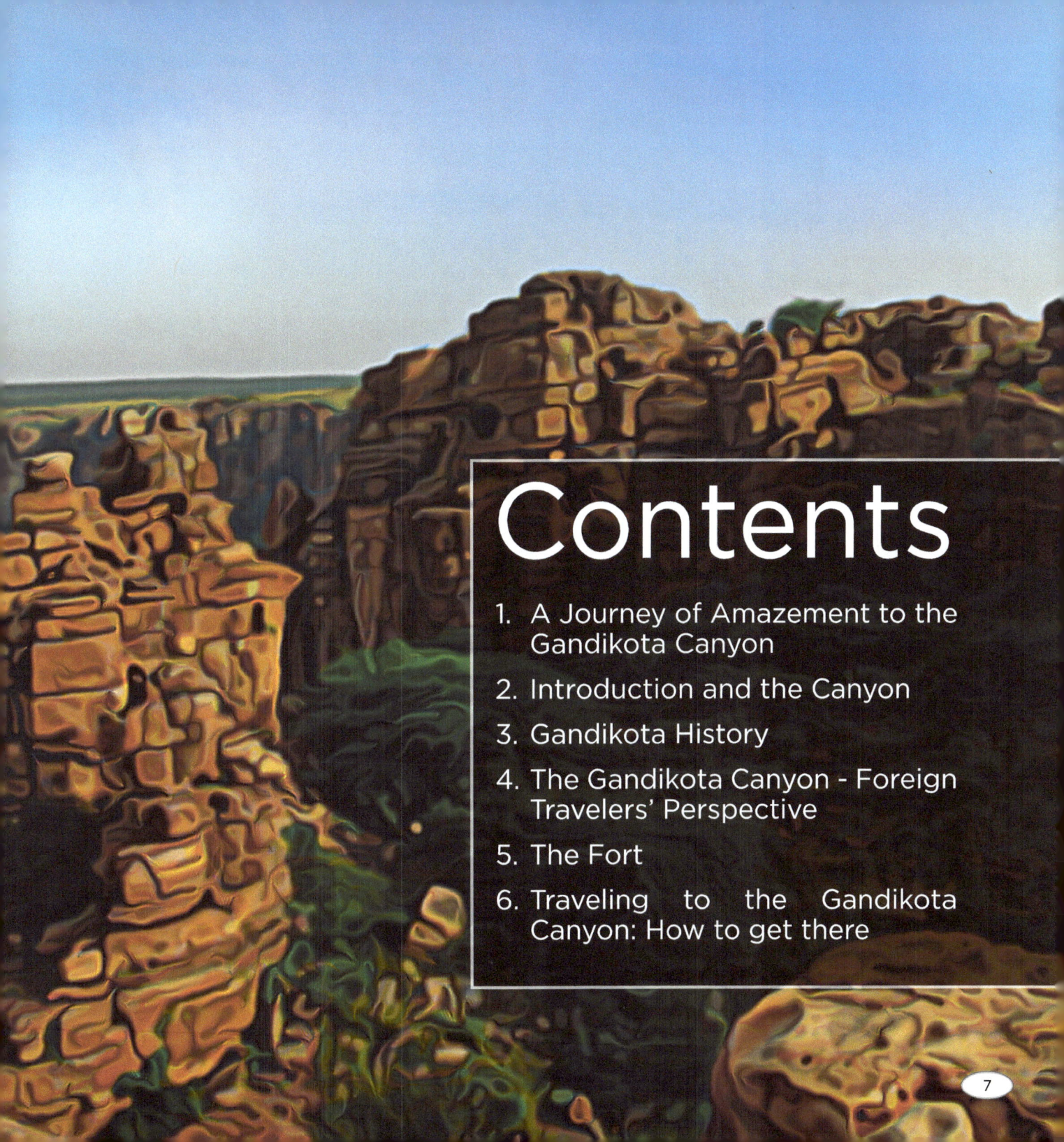

Contents

01 A JOURNEY OF AMAZEMENT TO THE GANDIKOTA CANYON

Picture: Karthik Kumar, Wikimedia Commons

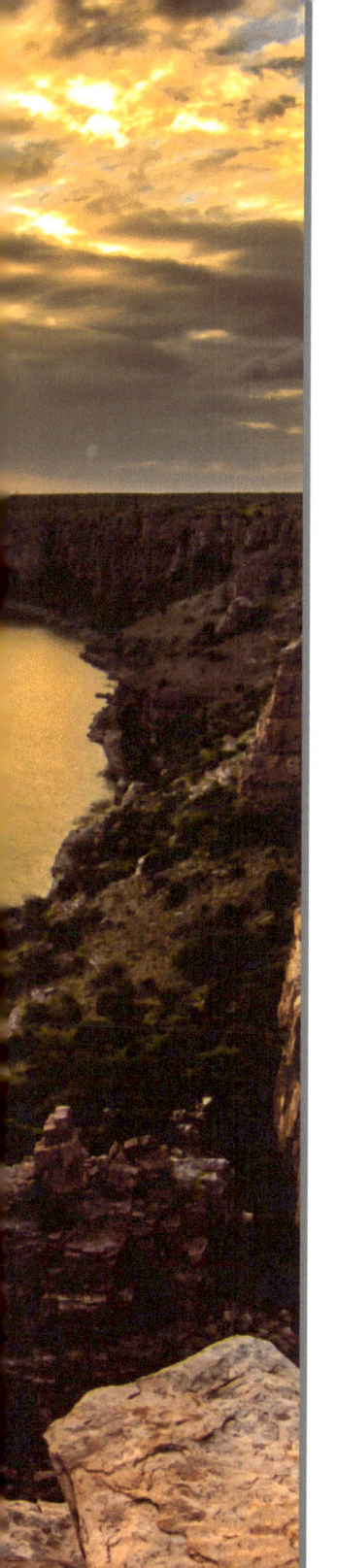

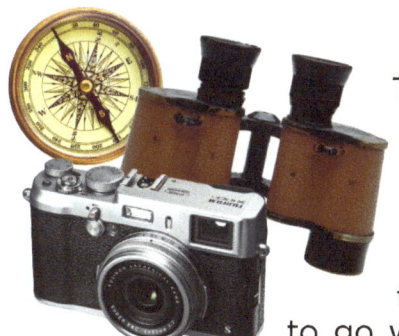

They say life is what happens to us while we are busy making other plans. This is so true in my case. I've always wanted to travel and write about my experiences, but it was difficult to do so. As an entrepreneur, the decision to travel was easy, but to decide on where to go was not! I'm not someone who follows travel trends or keeps up with Buzzfeed's latest 'Top 10 Destinations.'

I decided to freeze it down to our country first—India. Then, I decided to explore my part of the country—South India. This made my task easier; I was no longer overwhelmed with choices... or so I thought. The South is so vast. Should I start with beaches or spice plantations or the hill stations or places of pilgrimage? I took baby steps.

And then I came across some pictures of a gorge in the Kadapa district of Andhra Pradesh, and I could not believe this place existed in our country. It looked like a mini Grand Canyon (USA). I was intrigued enough to research further. The more I read up on the place, the more I wanted to experience it for myself to believe that it was actually true. Thus started my journey of amazement to Gandikota Canyon.

I did some web research on Gandikota before I set out. I'm a bit cautious, so I read books, searched bookshops for maps, met up with travel agents, got information on hotel rates, booking them, etc. This book is a record of my journey. It starts with geographical data, then historical—of national and international significance—and finally the nitty-gritty of the actual travel.

I hope readers find this book useful and that it inspires them to travel to Gandikota Canyon and other natural marvels in our country. I have clicked some of the pictures in the book, and some have been sourced from Wikipedia, Wikitravel, Wikiwand and Wikimedia.

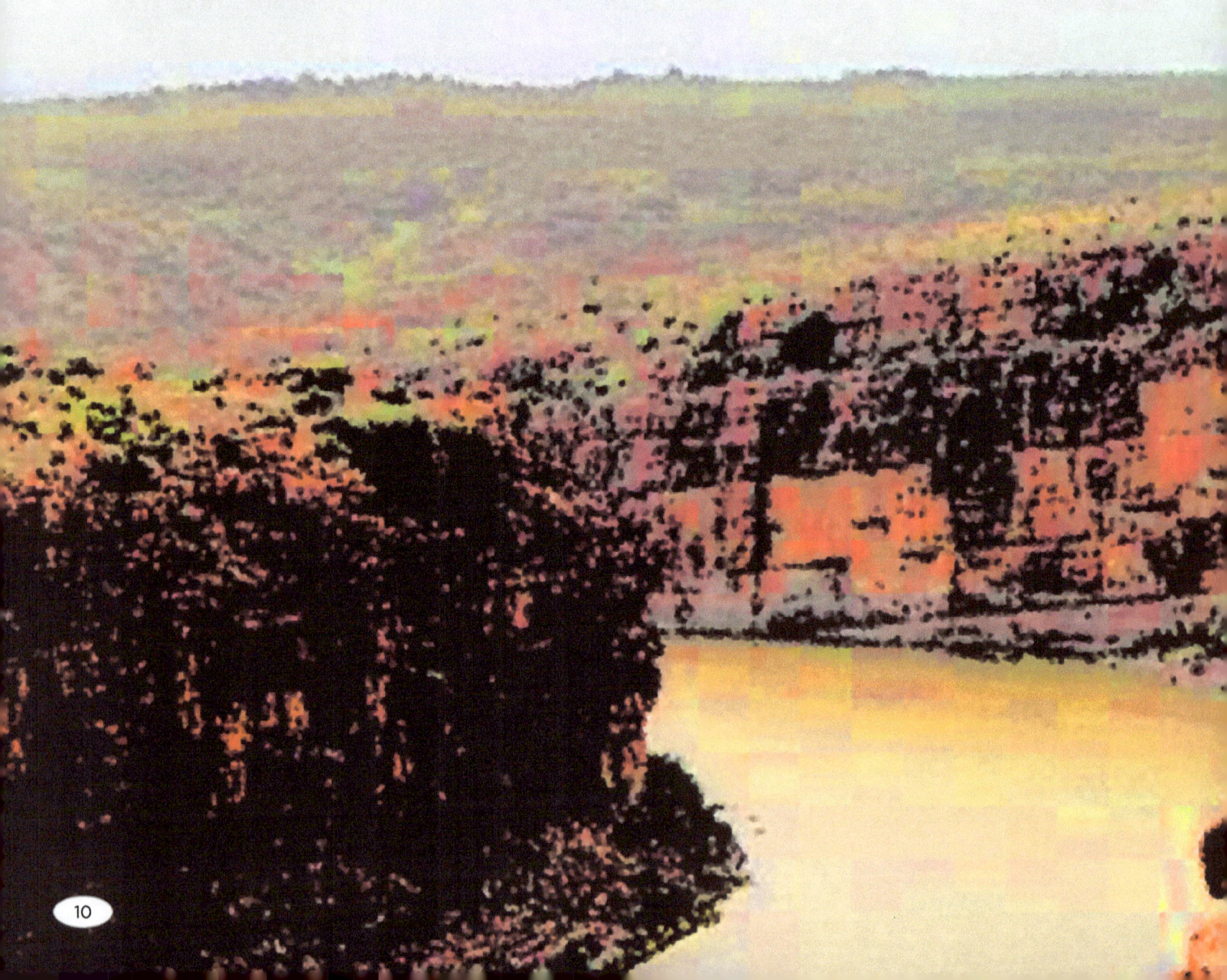

02 INTRODUCTION AND THE CANYON

Gandikota Canyon

Gandikota is a village nestled on the banks of the river Pennar. It is located 16 km from Jammalamadugu in Kadapa district of Andhra Pradesh, India.

The word *'gandi'* means 'gorge' and the word *'kota'* means 'fort' or 'fortification' in Telegu, the official language of Andhra Pradesh. Therefore, the fort is called 'Gandikota'—the fort of the gorge. The village surrounding it has taken its name from the fort.

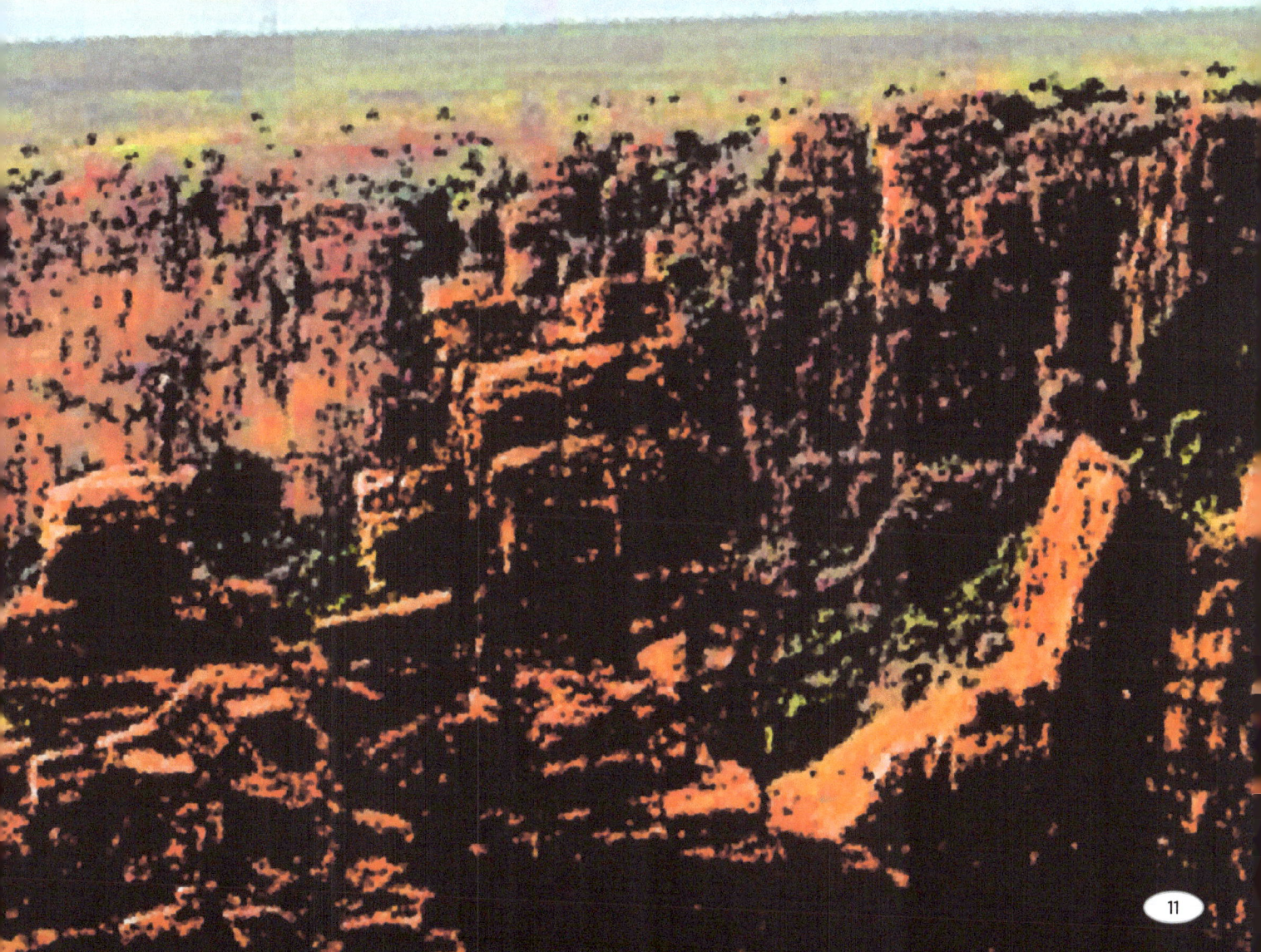

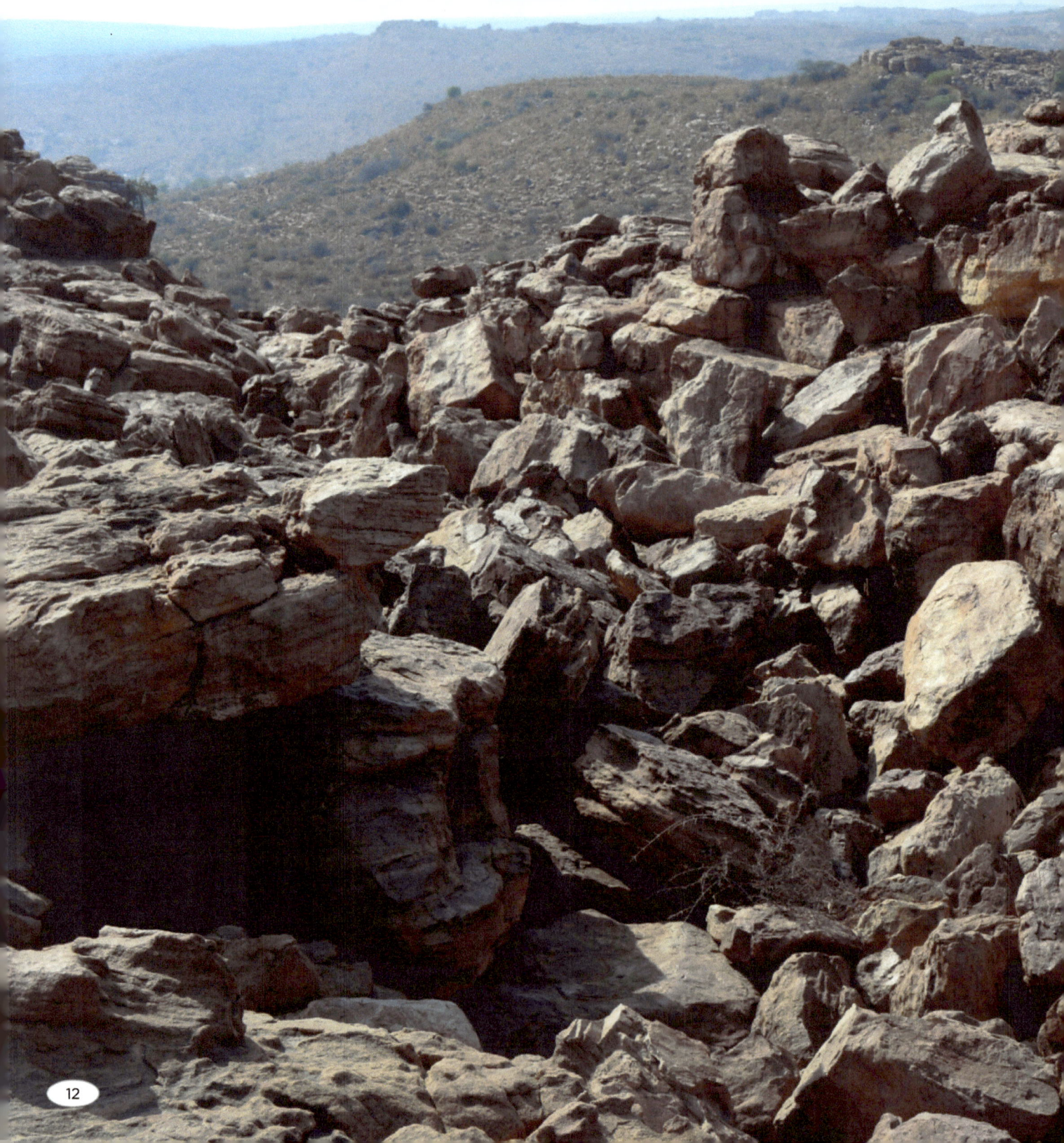

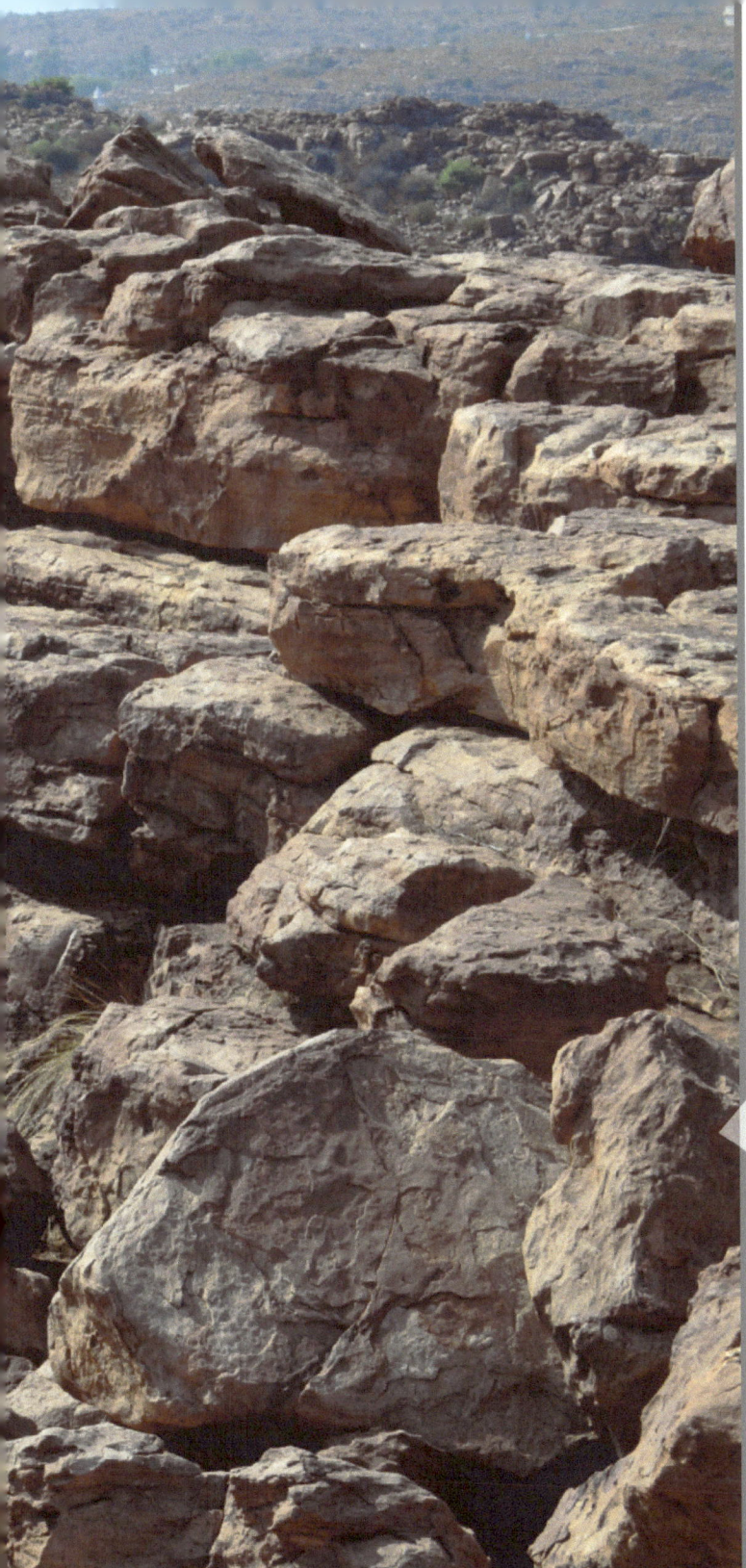

The geography of Gandikota is fascinating, and not just to geologists. Any layperson can tell that he or she is in the midst of a natural wonder.

The Gandikota Fort is situated between the Erramala range of hills and the river Pennar. The river flows at the foothills and is a mere 300 feet wide. Pennar has cut through the hills, creating a magnificent gorge.

The Gandikota Fort complex has two temples and one masjid inside—the Madhavaraya Temple, the Ranganatha Swamy Temple, and the Jama Masjid.

Gandikota Canyon is a part of the Cuddapah Basin. The Cuddapah Basin is on the eastern margin of the Dharwar Craton. It is the largest Proterozoic basin in South India.

Geologist **P.D. Sabale** explains how the Gandikota Canyon was formed.

"The river Pennar cuts the Pink Granite, which forms the bedrock here. While it's not an easy process to cut an igneous, acidic, tough and compact mass of granite, the natural decomposition of the rock made it weather fast."

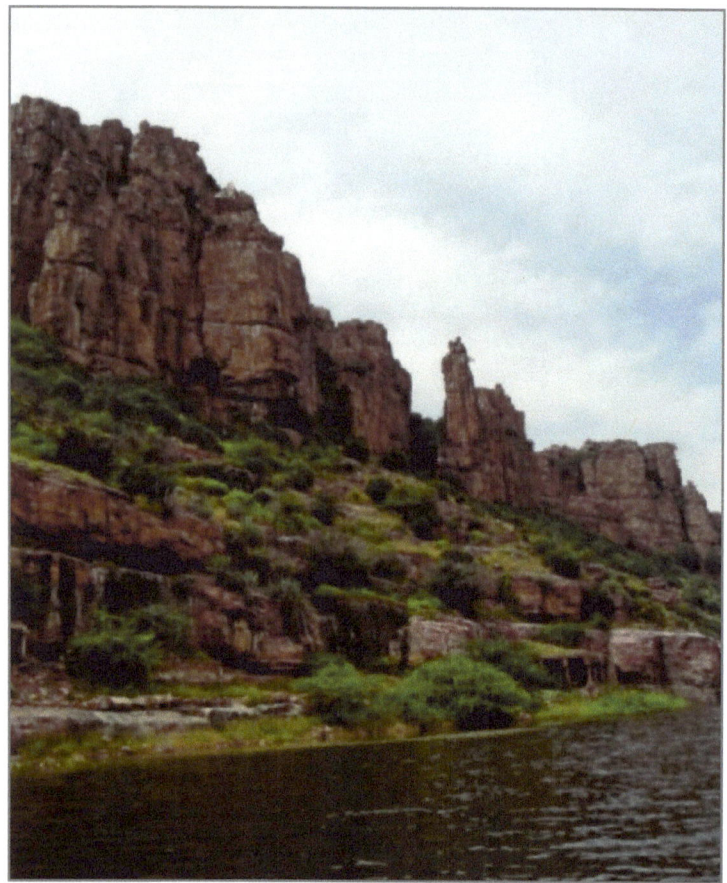
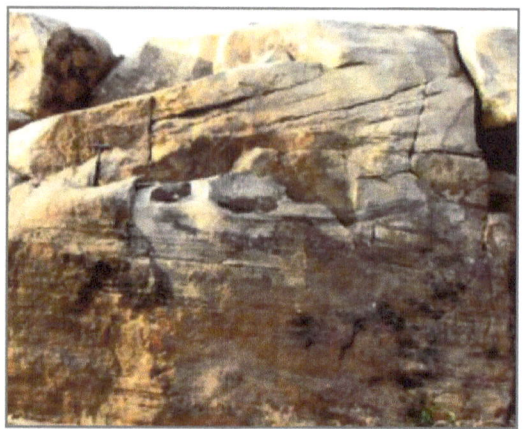
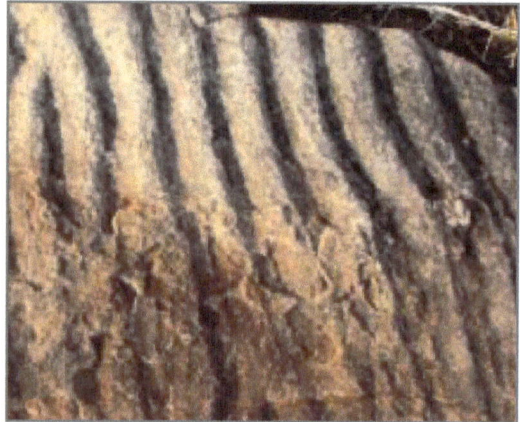

1 Craton is an old and stable part of the continental lithosphere, where the lithosphere consists of the Earth's two topmost layers: the crust and the uppermost mantle. Cratons survive cycles of merging and rifting of continents and are found in the interiors of tectonic plates. They are made of ancient crystalline basement rock, which may be covered by younger sedimentary rock. They have a thick crust and deep lithospheric roots that extend sometimes several hundred kilometres into the Earth's mantle.

2 Proterozoic is a geological eon spanning the time from the appearance of oxygen in the Earth's atmosphere to just before the proliferation of complex life (such as trilobites or corals) on Earth. The Proterozoic Eon extended from 2500 MYA (million years ago) to 541 MYA. It is the longest eon of the Earth's geologic time scale.

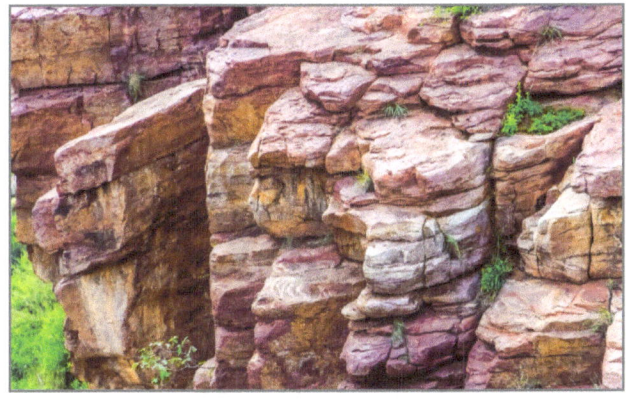
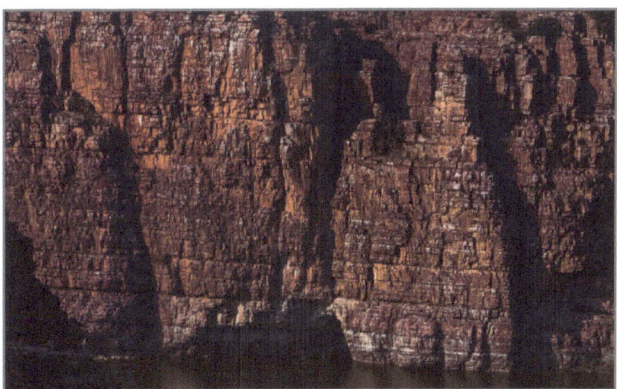
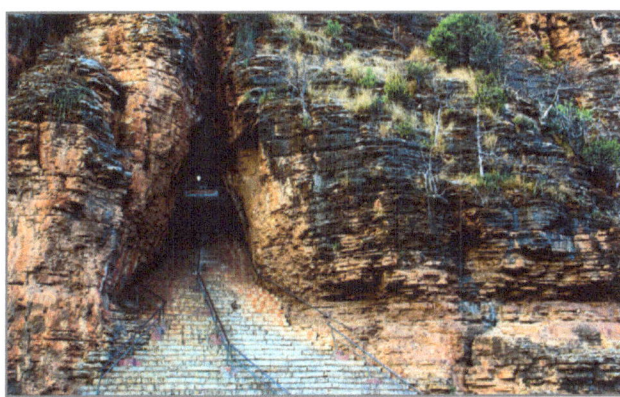
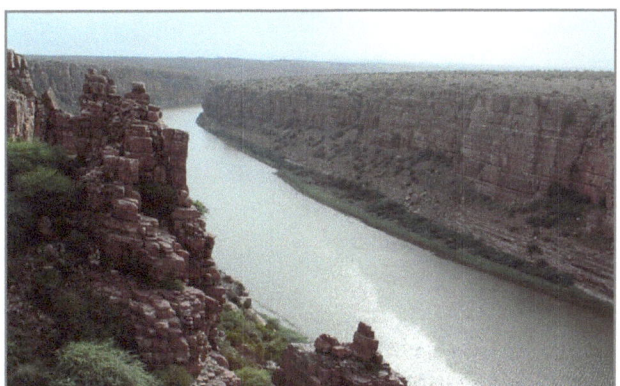

This makes Gandikota one of the oldest natural formations on Earth. Of course, the Indian subcontinent is a very ancient land with many more ancient formations. We often take this for granted and overlook the treasures that reside in our backyards.

The Gandikota Canyon is made up of intrusive igneous rock. Igneous rock (derived from the Latin word *ignis* meaning fire), or magmatic rock, is one of the three main rock types found on Earth.

Igneous rock is formed through the cooling and solidification of magma or lava.

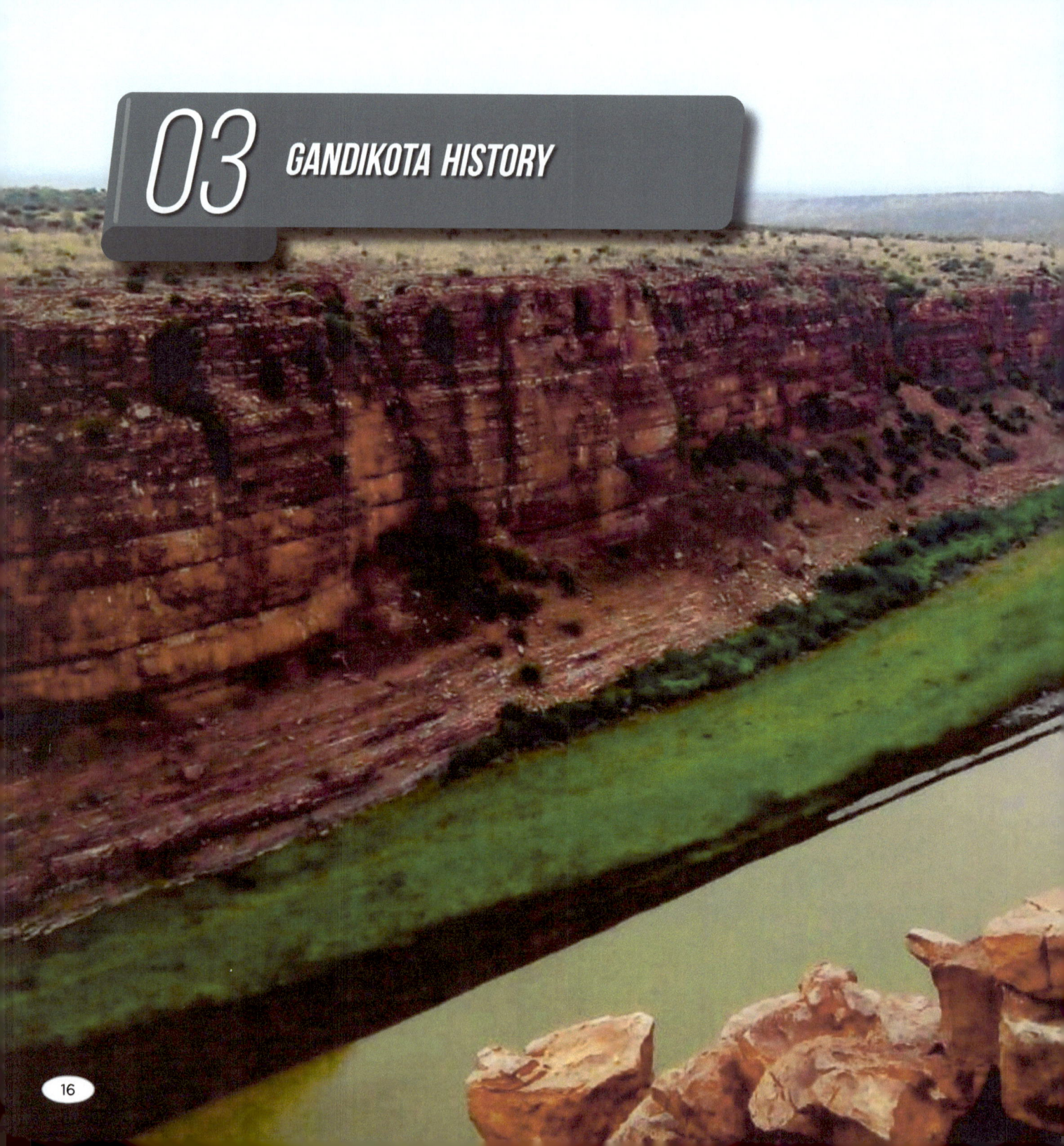

03 GANDIKOTA HISTORY

The history of Gandikota is quite illustrious. It was first identified as a strategic area and made into a sand fort in 1123 by Kapa Raja of Bommanapalle. Kapa Raja was a subordinate of Ahavamalla Someswara I, the Western Chalukyan king of Kalyana.

However, the village of Gandikota transformed into a major fortified area only after the emergence of the Pemmasani Nayaks. Pemmasani Nayaks were a Kamma clan (Kamma is a caste found in South India, especially Andhra Pradesh and Tamil Nadu). They came into prominence as feudatories of Gandikota under the rule of the Vijayanagar kings.

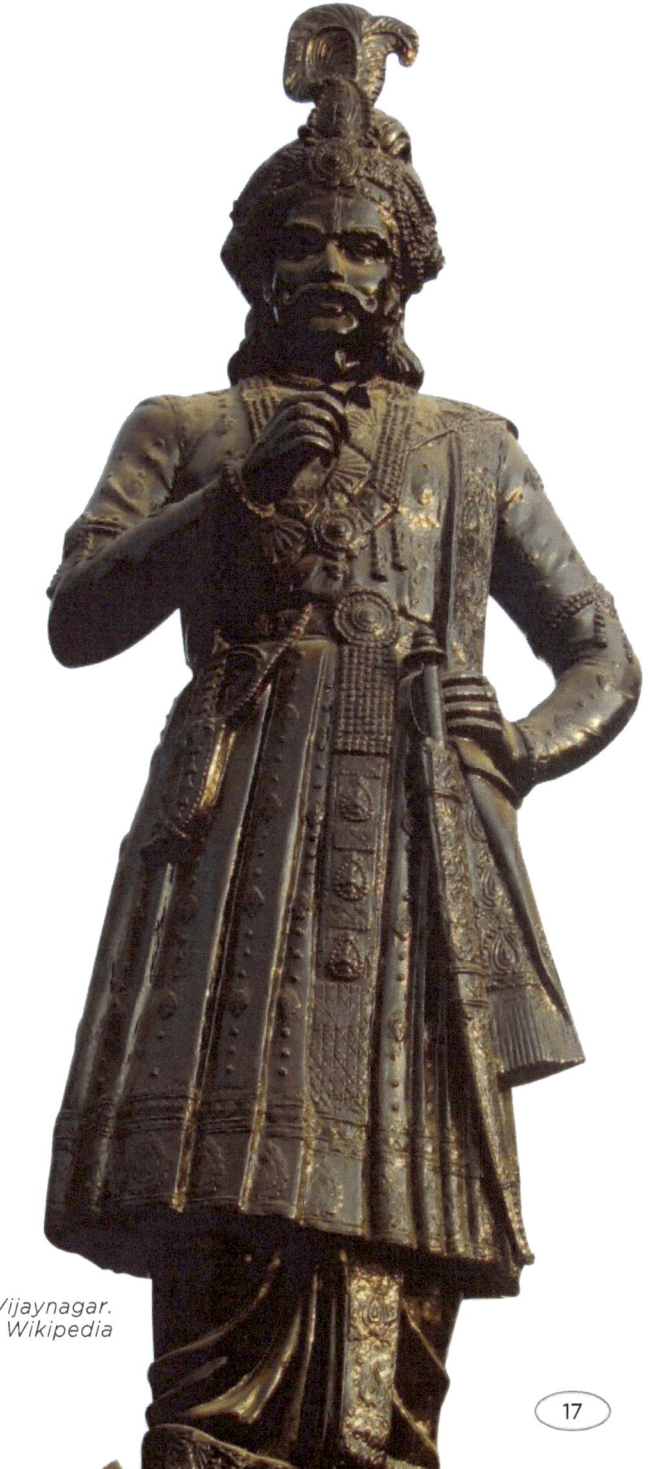

Statue of Krishna Deva Raya in Vijaynagar.
Image courtesy Wikipedia

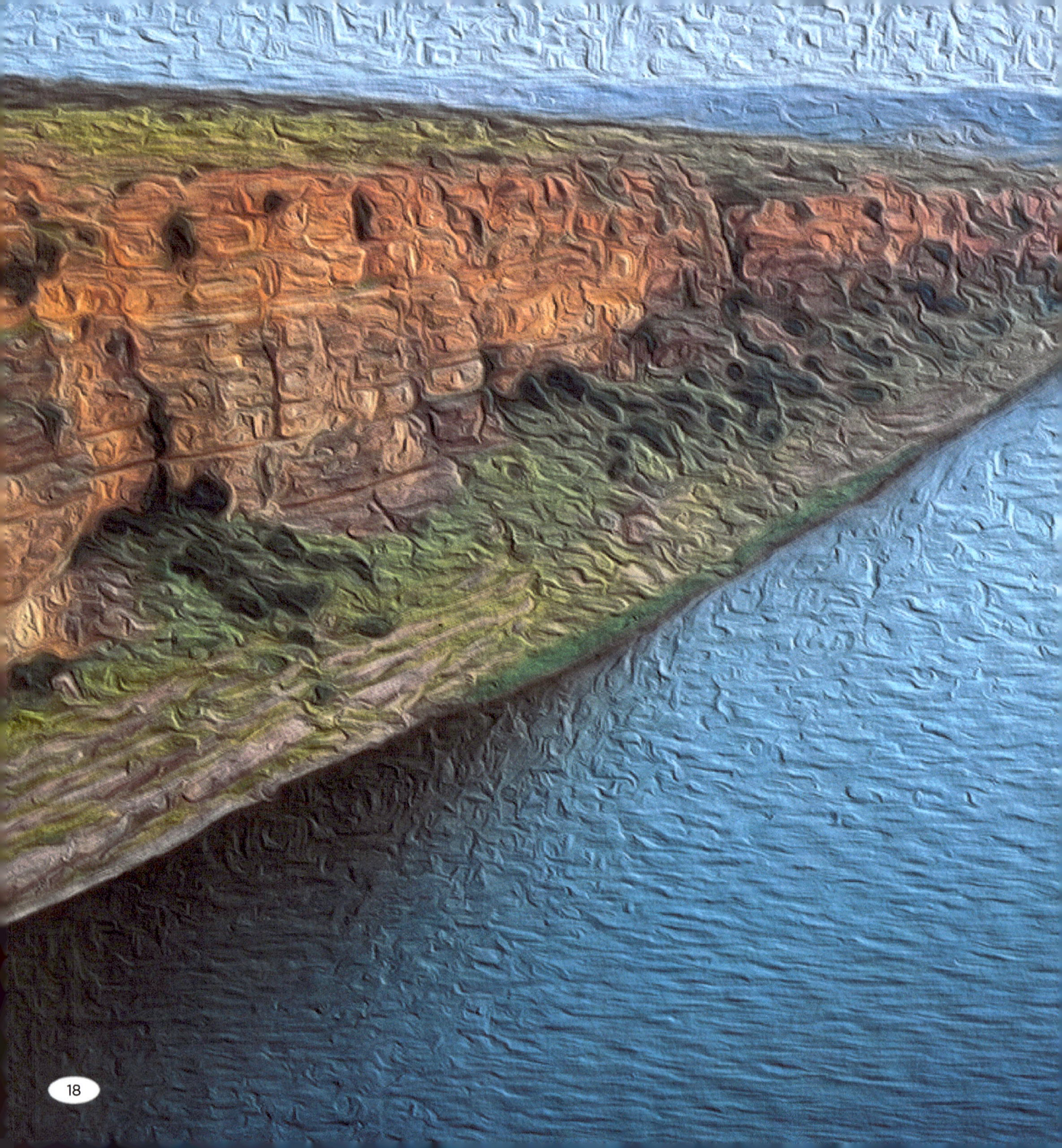

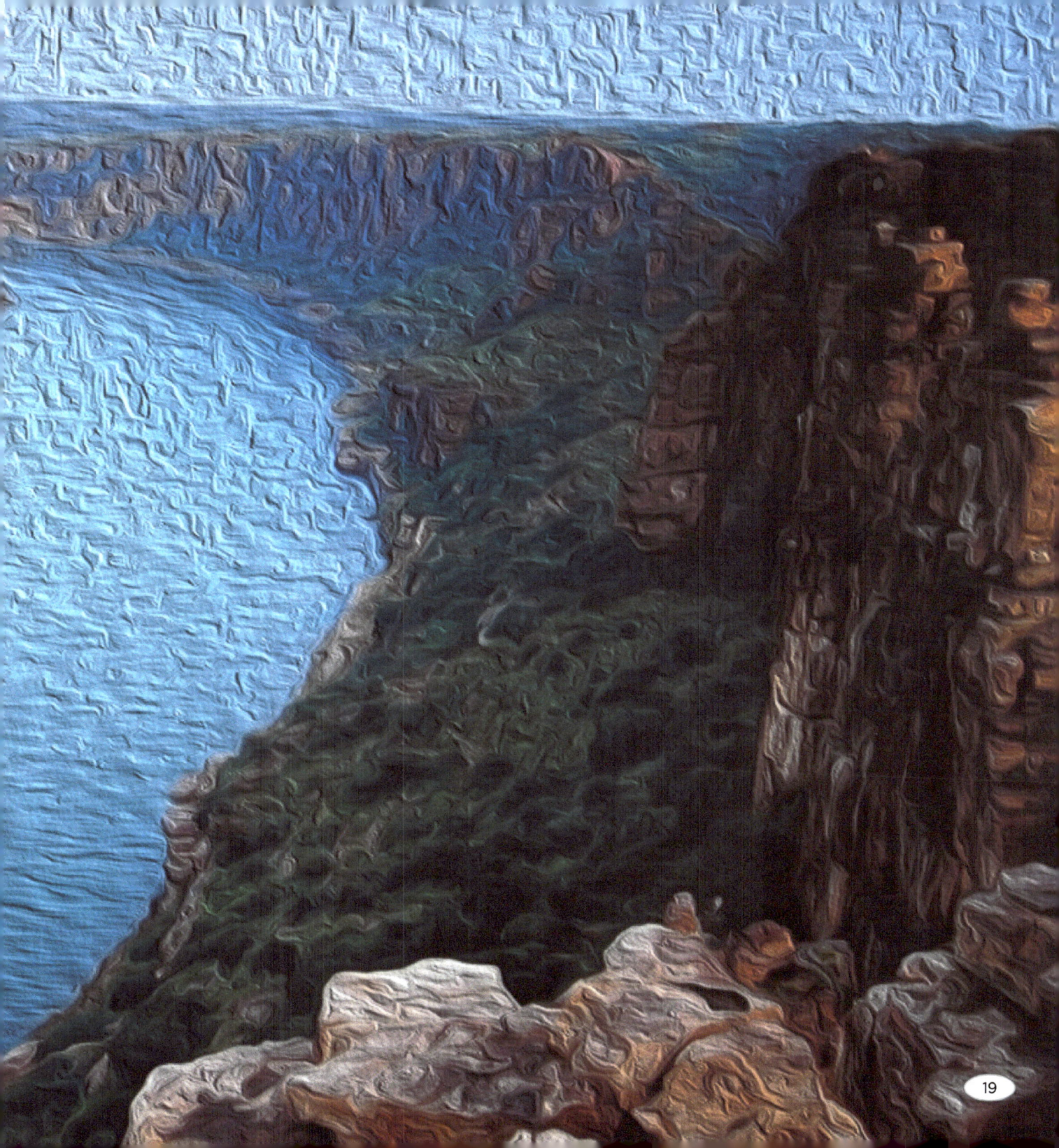

THE GANDIKOTA CANYON
FOREIGN TRAVELERS' PERSPECTIVE

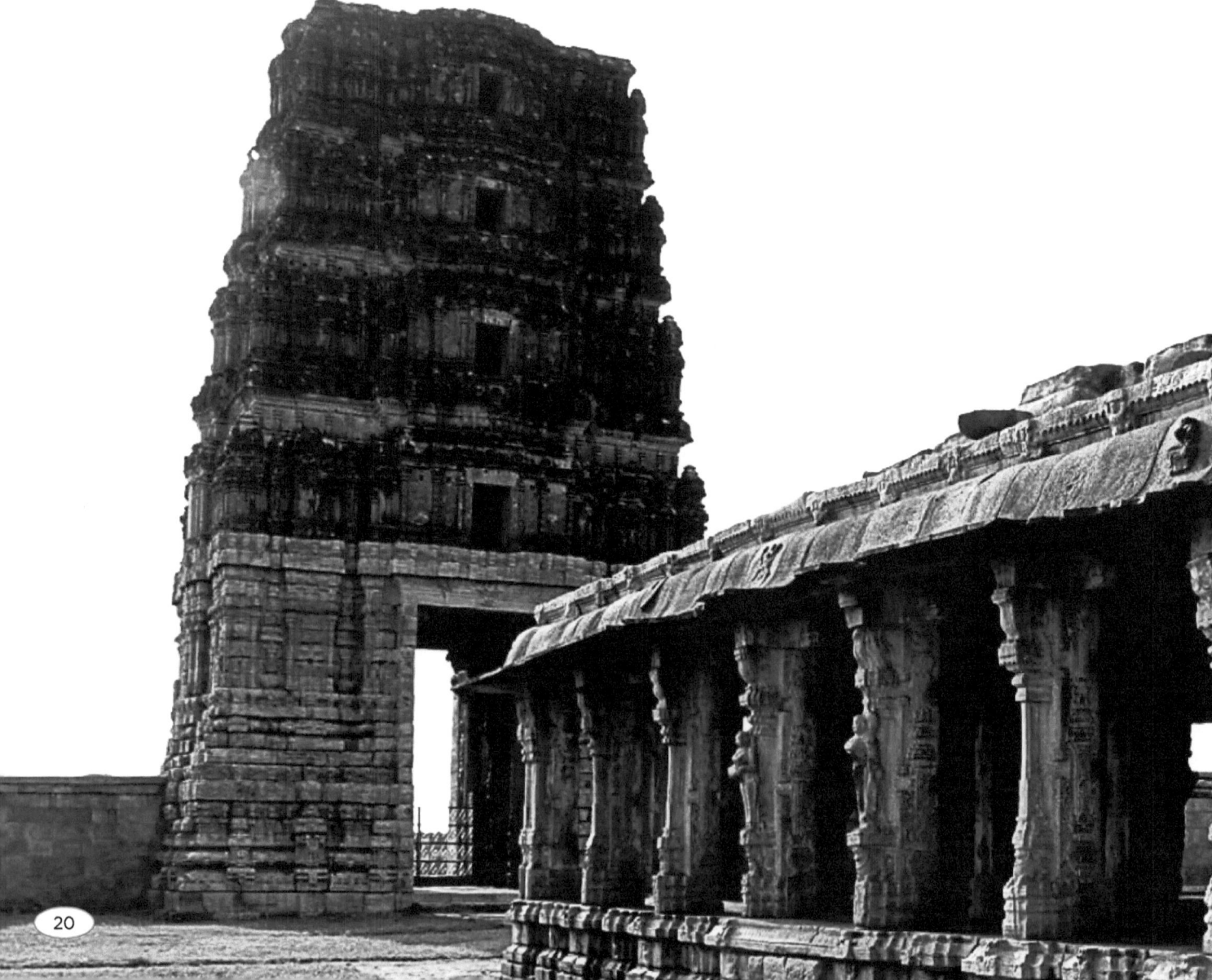

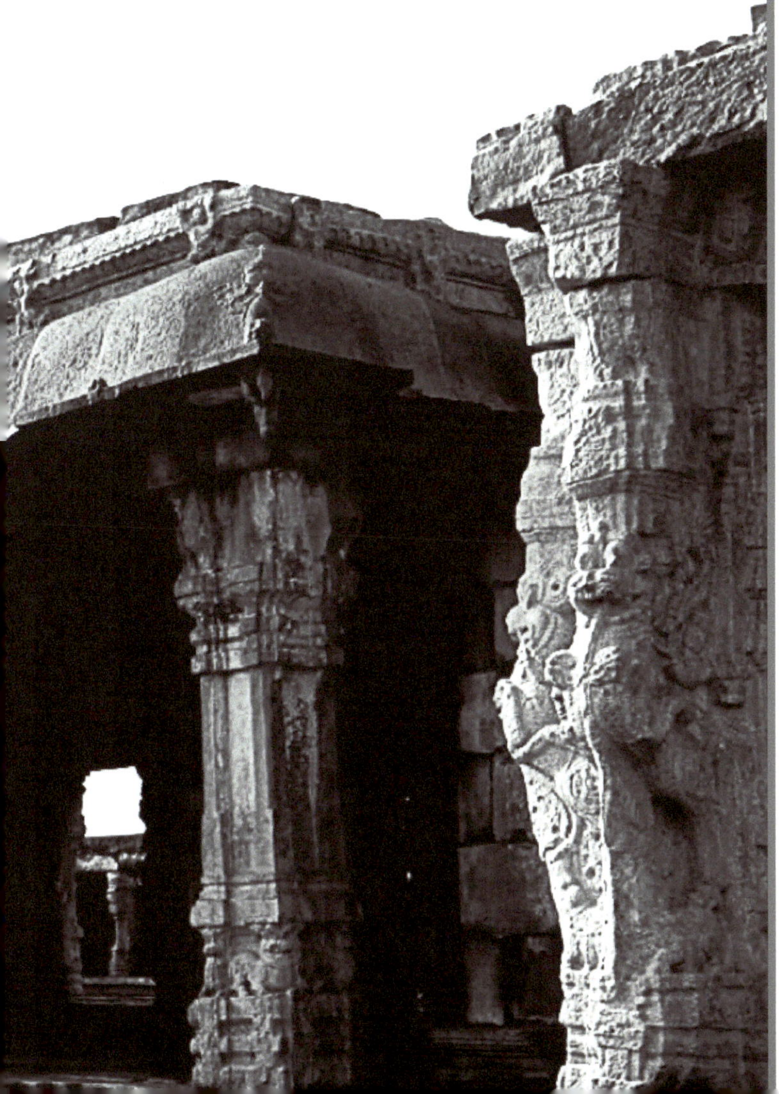

Long before there were calls in Andhra Pradesh to push for a 'UNESCO World Heritage Site' status for the Gandikota complex of fort, masjid and temples overlooking the canyon; it had inspired and amazed several world travelers.

Notable among these was a French gem merchant and traveler, Jean-Baptiste Tavernier (1605-1689). Tavernier traveled at his own expense, making six voyages to Persia and India between the years 1630 and 1668. He chronicled his expeditions in the book *Les Six Voyages de Jean-Baptiste Tavernier (Six Voyages*, 1676). He was encouraged to publish by his patron, King Louis XIV.

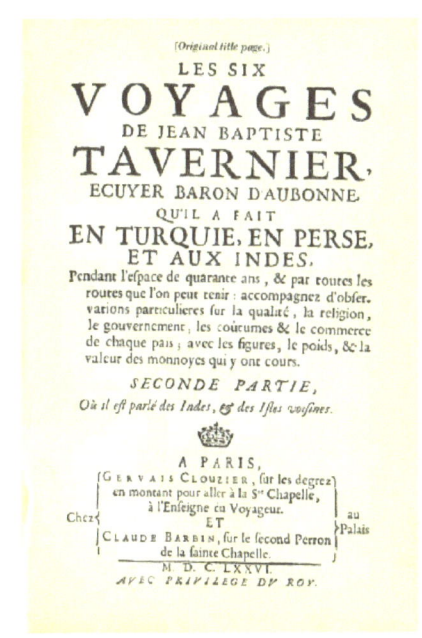

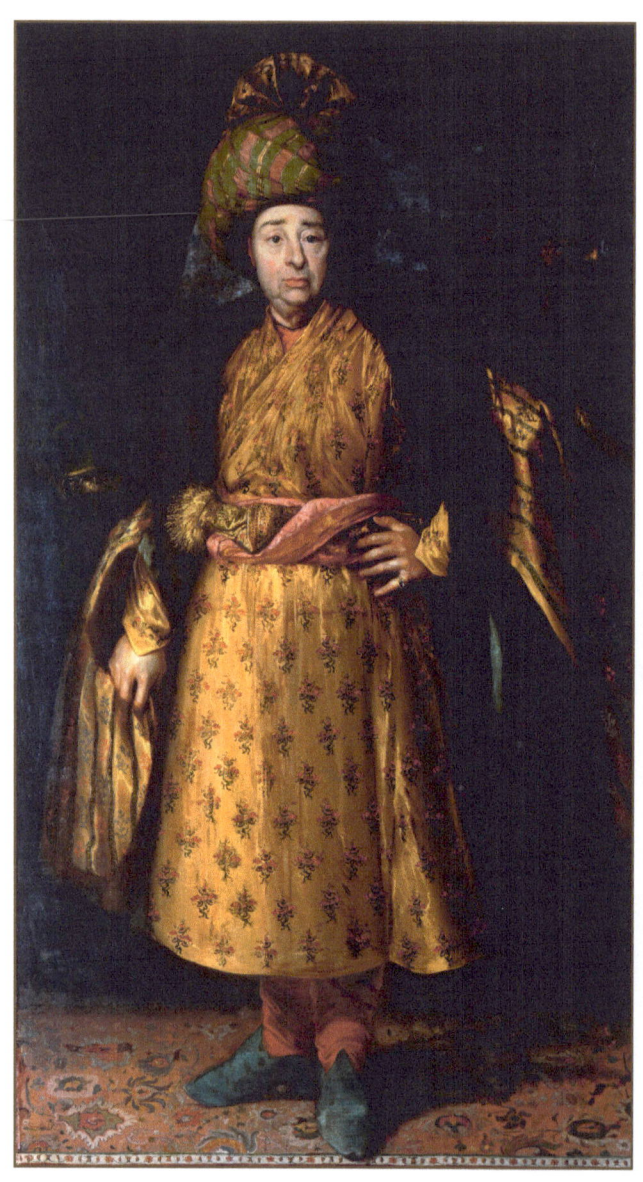

*Jean-Baptiste Tavernier in oriental
costume by Nicolas de Largillière, 1679.
Image courtesy Wikipedia*

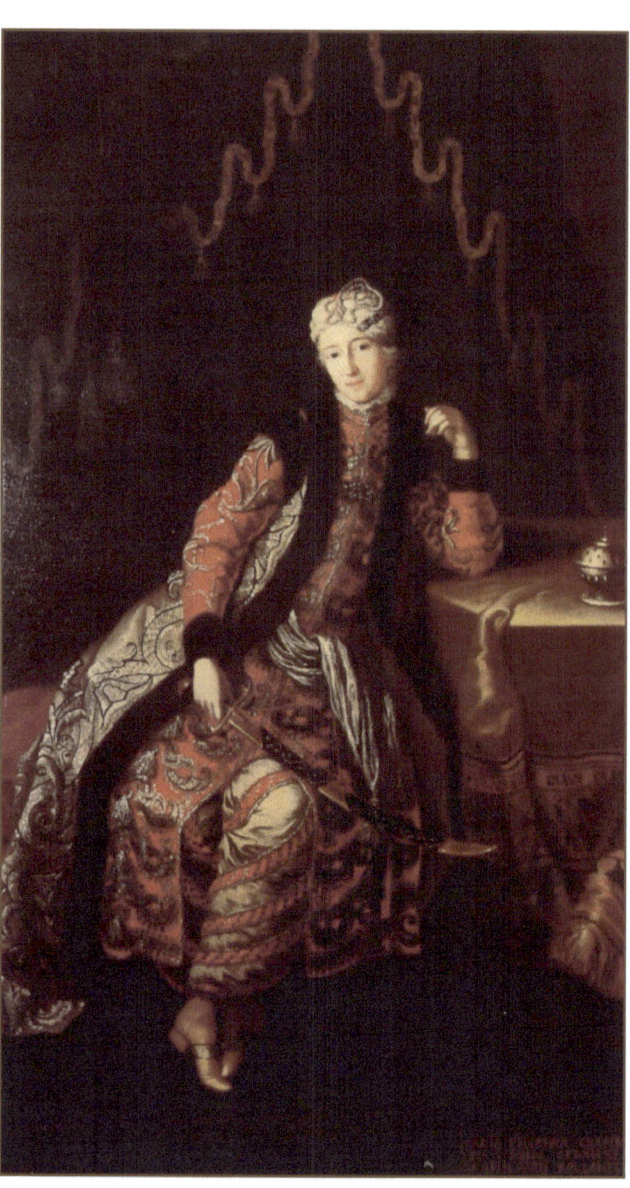

*Portrait of Tavernier
by Nicolas de Largillière, 1700.
Image courtesy Wikipedia*

Tavernier was born in a family of cartographers; his father Gabriel and his uncle Melchior were skilled in the trade, and they seem to have trained Tavernier too, as is evident from the accuracy and technical finesse of Tavernier's drawings of his journeys.

But Tavernier was struck by wanderlust, and even as a teenager, he had traveled extensively through Europe and was proficient in several major European languages. He reminds one of today's teenagers making Instagram memories as they travel— except he carefully illustrated and engraved his experiences.

Of his six journeys, the second one was in September 1638, lasting till 1643. Tavernier traveled via Aleppo to Persia and from there to India. He went to Agra and to the Kingdom of Golconda. He visited the court of the great Mogul Emperor Shah Jahan and made his first trip to the diamond mines.

This is what Tavernier says about Gandikota in his book:

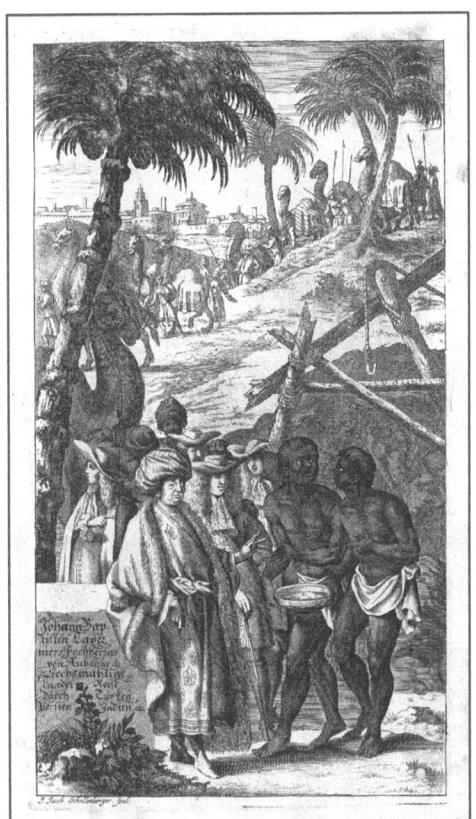

Gandikota is one of the fortified towns in the Kingdom of *Carnatic*. It is built on the summit of a high mountain, and the sole means of access to it is by a very difficult road, which is only 20 or 25 feet wide, and in certain parts only 7 or 8; the Nawab was then commencing to improve it. On the right of the road, which is cut in the mountain, there is a fearful precipice, at the base of which runs a large river [the Penner]. On the top of the mountain there is a small plain about a quarter of a league wide and a half a league long. It is cultivated with rice and millet, and watered by many small springs. At the level of the plain to the south, where the town is built on a point, the limits are formed by precipices, with two rivers which bound the point at the base; so that, for access to the town, there is but one gate on the plain side, and it is fortified in that direction with three good walls of cut stone, the ditches at their bases being faced with the same stone.

Illustration by Tavernier of his journeys in the Orient, meeting the natives

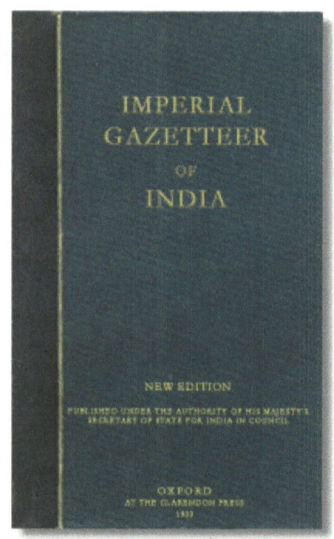

This is what The Imperial Gazetteer of India by Sir William Stevenson Meyer 1860-1922, page 127 has to say. about Gandikota. Sir William Stevenson Meyer (13 February 1860 - 19 October 1922) was an Indian Civil Service officer. From 1920 until his death two years later, he served as the first High Commissioner for India.

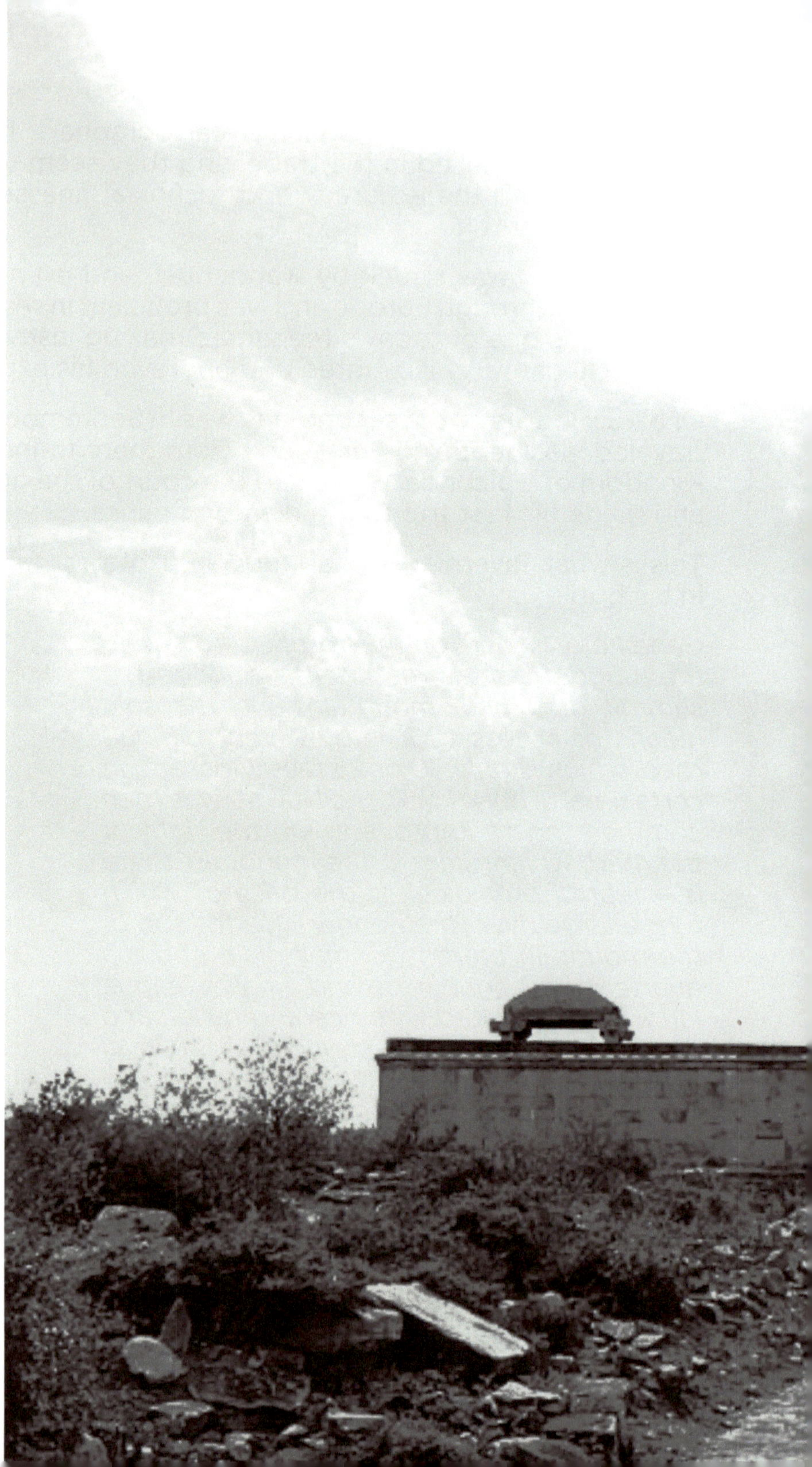

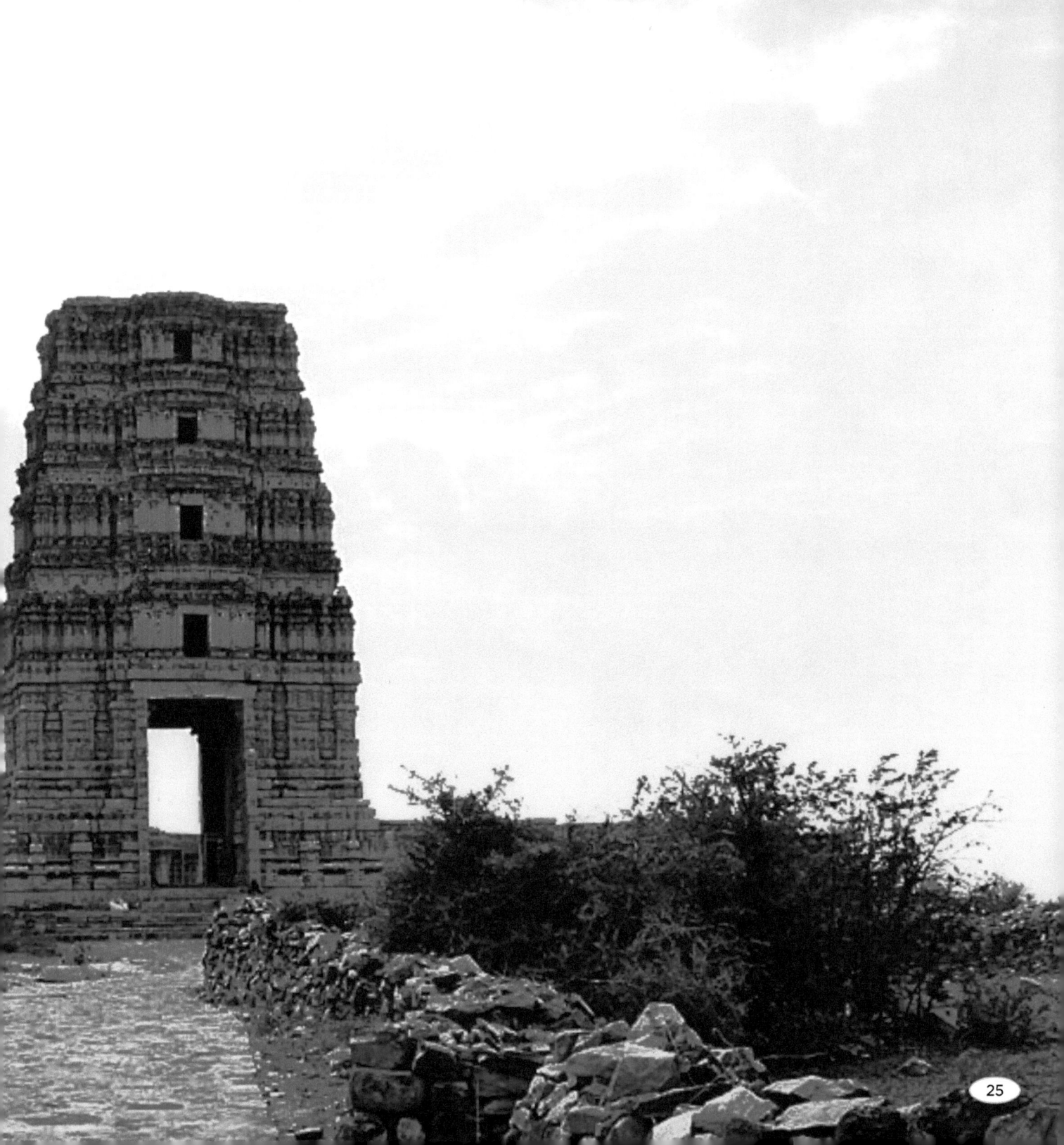

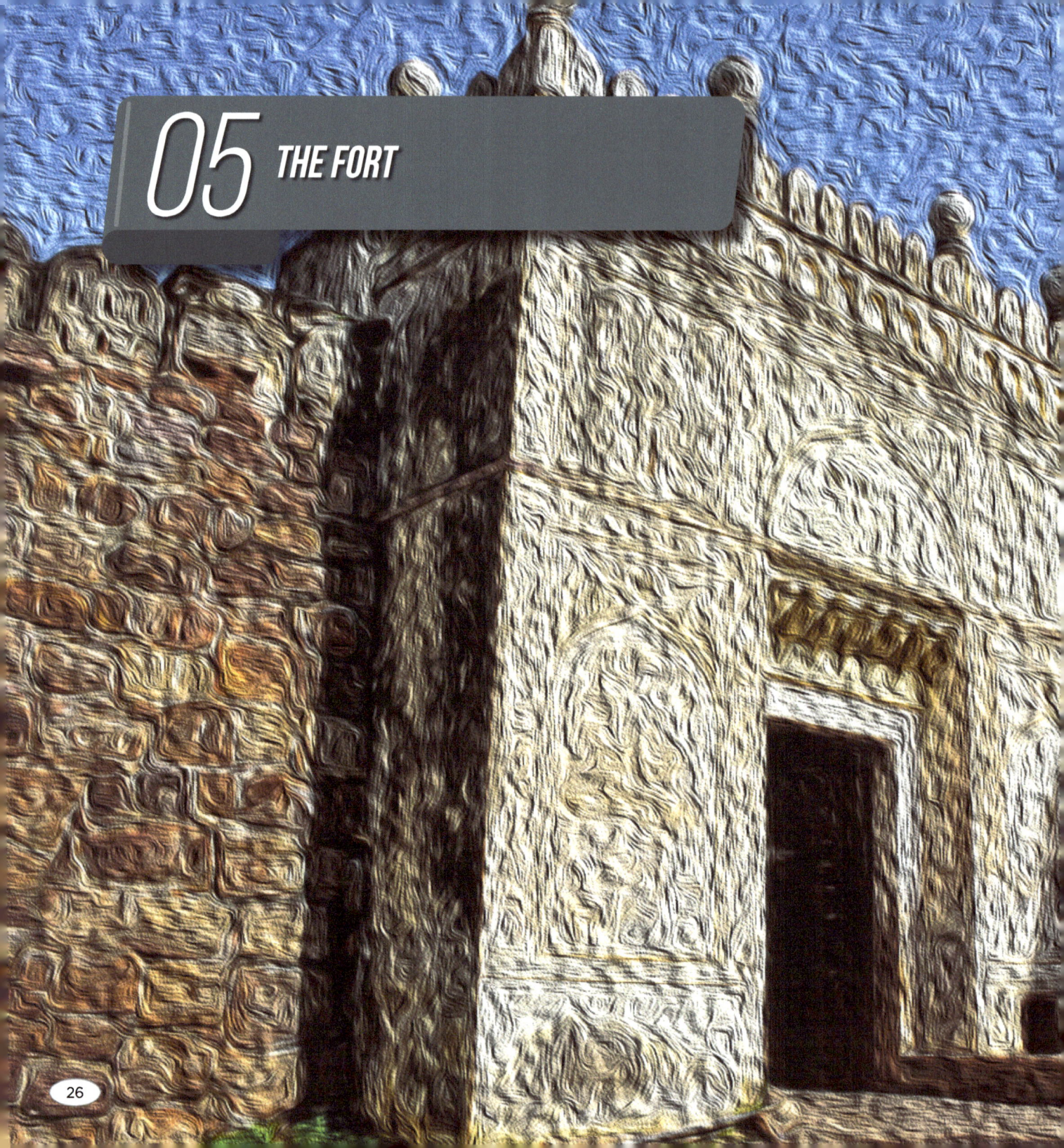

05 THE FORT

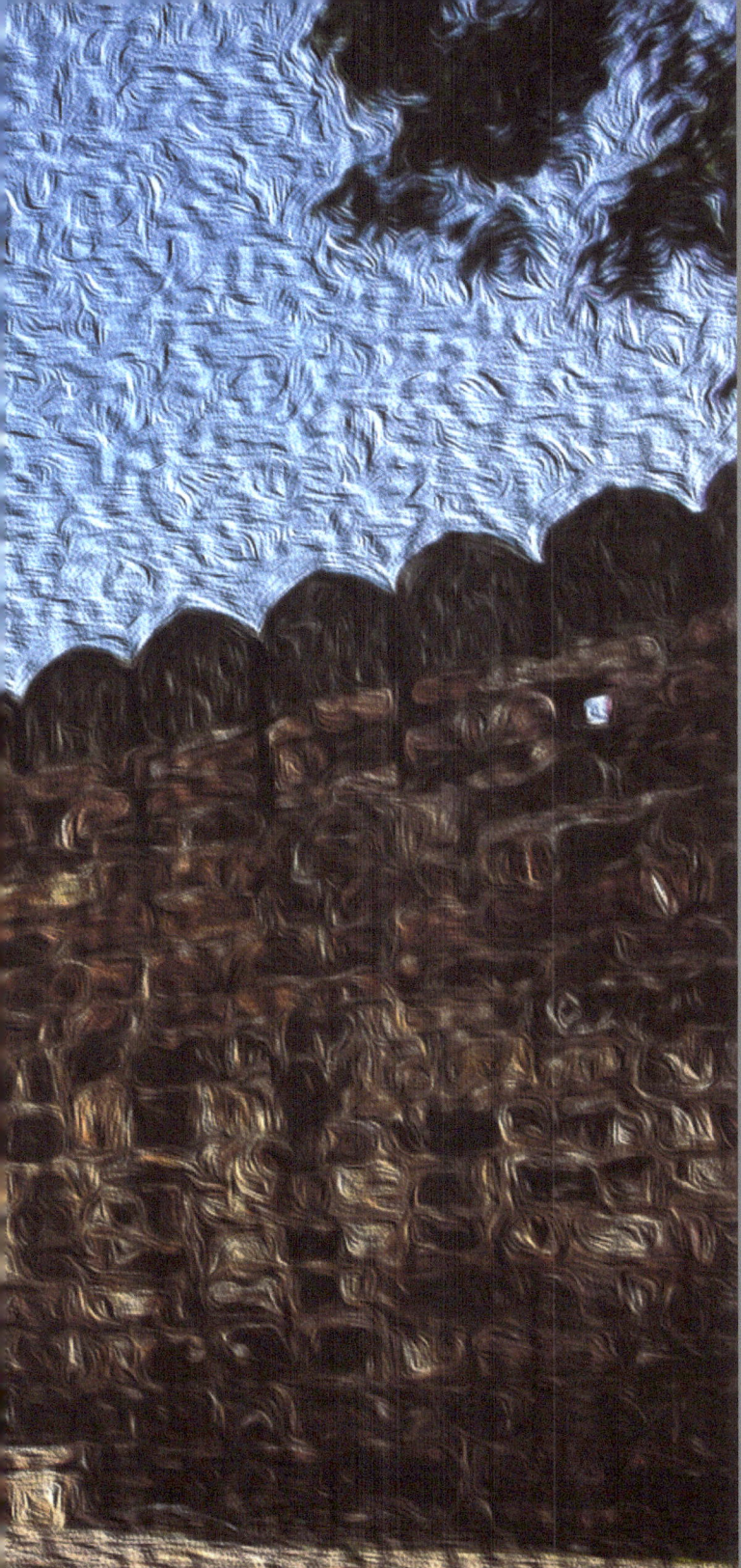

It is said that the Gandikota Fort complex is among South India's most well-planned fortified complexes. With its strategic location on a gorge caused in the Eramalla hill range by the river Pennar cutting through, the fort was much sought after for its vantage position.

Standing on the ramparts of the fort even today it is easy to see why. It is a vast, flat tableland, with a clear, unobstructed view as the Pennar winds its way into the horizon. The raw material required to build strong forts was typically transported from distant places, but in this case, it was right here—the large living rocks. The river, which nourishes the otherwise arid landscape, was pulled into the fort complex and the village through an elaborate system of aqueducts and aquifers.

Armed with this knowledge gleaned from government tourism websites, newspaper articles and internet blogs, I set out for Gandikota. I had been planning this trip for a long time. In fact, I had collected way too much information. And the information overload led to an action paralysis! I took things too easy, feeling like I already knew the place and how to get there. Needless to say, my journey started off quite disastrously, having awakened an hour later than the scheduled time of departure, with no packing done and my tourist taxi running late, and

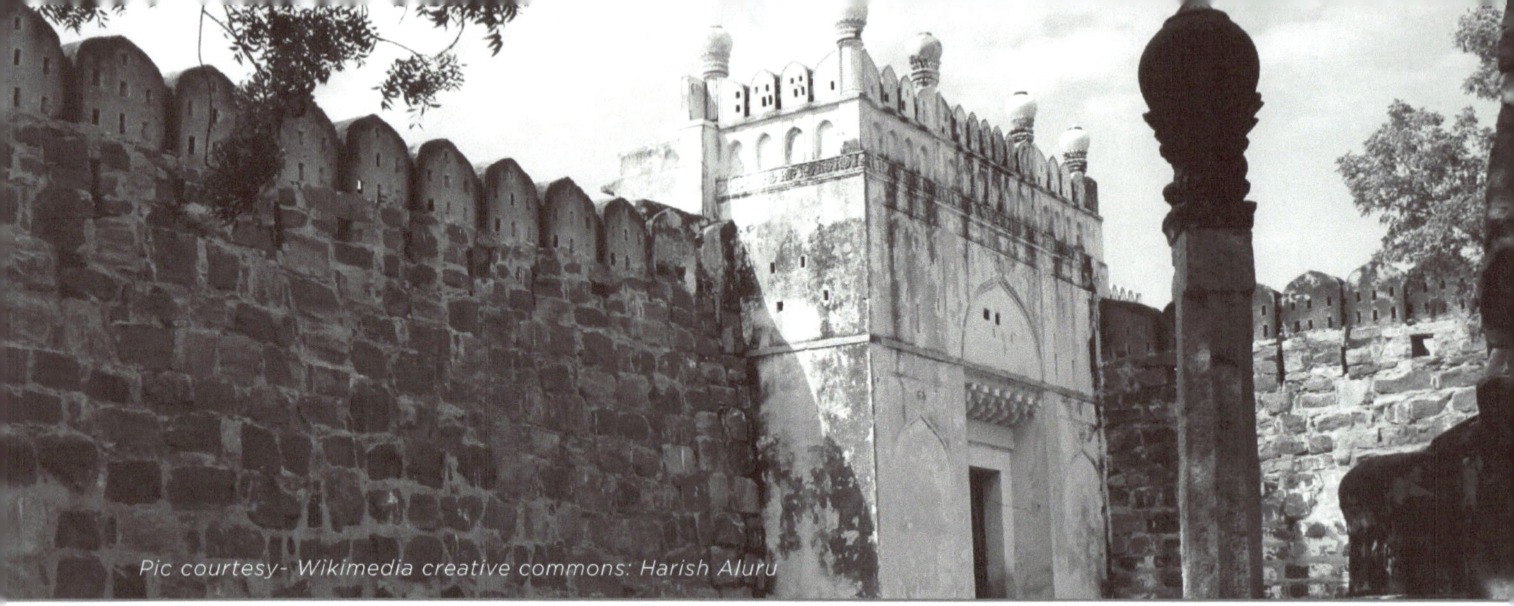

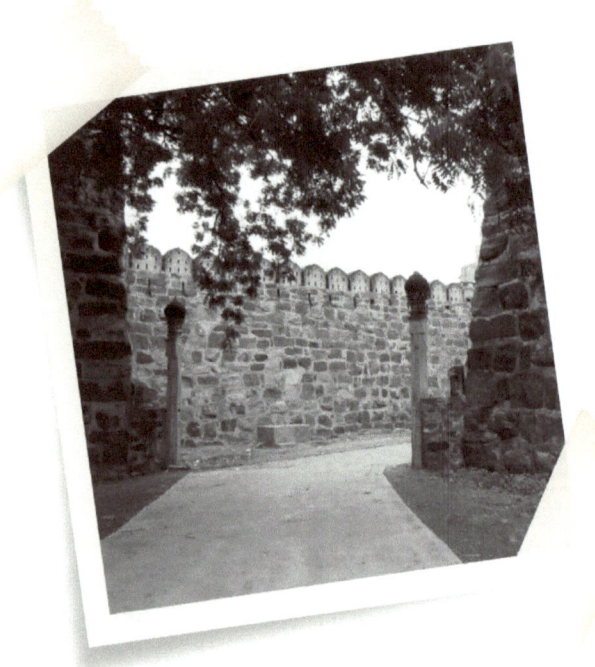

I had also skipped breakfast. After eight hours of traveling on an empty stomach, I finally arrived at Gandikota. Like those fabled weary warriors would have after battles ages ago.

As soon as I entered the fort complex, the massive walls of red stone made me realize how impenetrable this fort must have been in its heyday. The entrance itself was imposing at 20 feet tall with a huge *darwaaza* of metal, replete with sharp spikes. It looked quite terrifying at first glance. The spikes had surely skewered many an unwanted visitor in olden times.

The other thing that struck me was that this was not some dead and dusty heritage preserved antiseptically for tourists to view; the fort was alive and humming with the activity of everyday life right before my eyes. Families were living inside and around the fort complex.

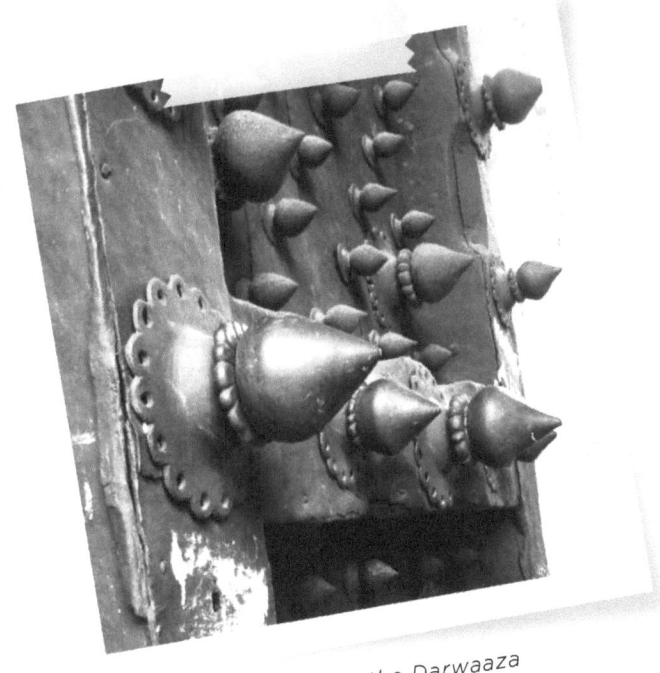

Spikes on the Darwaaza

The fort complex was an excellent example of the syncretic existence of the two religions in Andhra. There were two temples and a Jama Masjid that stood peacefully, cheek by jowl, in this complex. Both bore the rigors of pilferage and destruction in equal measure. One thing to note is that there is no specific order in which you can view the monuments. As a traveler, you are free to mix and match, choosing to see the masjid before the mandirs or the natural gorge before the man-made structures. Suit yourself, and let your mood take you along. The order I chose suited me. Also, keep in mind your timing. Early morning is always a good time, as there are fewer tourists. I landed up in the evening.

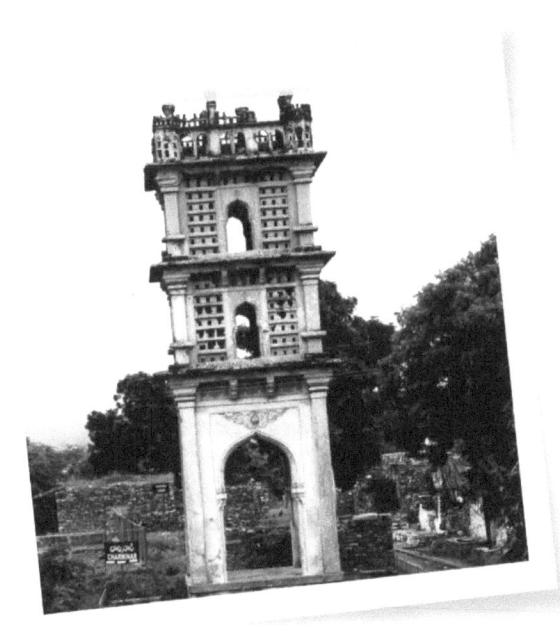

Charminar for pigeons

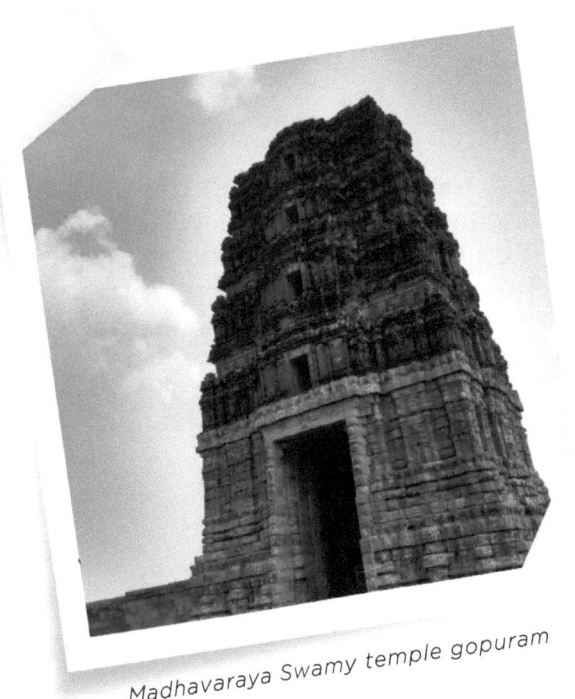

Madhavaraya Swamy temple gopuram

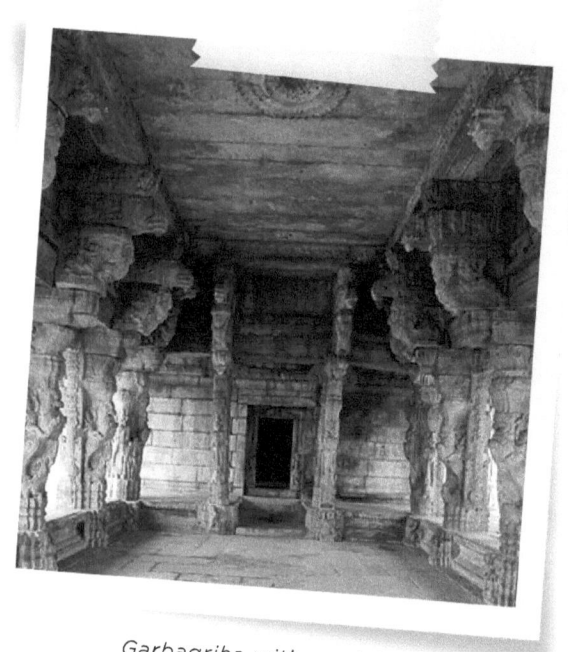

Garbagriha with no deity

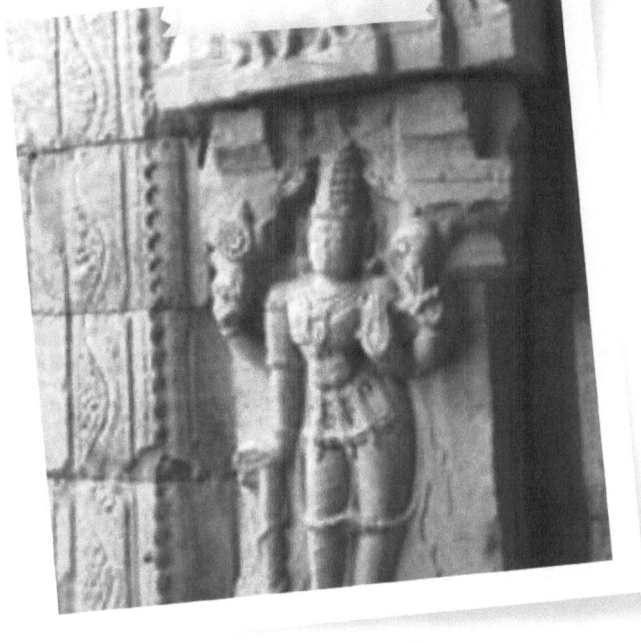

Carving on pillar

The first temple I visited in the complex was the Madhavaraya Swamy Temple. Its majestic and intricately carved *gopuram* was the tallest structure in the complex. In fact, it could be seen from quite a distance, almost acting like a beacon, drawing you into the complex. As I entered through the *gopuram,* the inside complex amazed me with its vast, open courtyard surrounded by elaborately carved pillars around the sanctum sanctorum in its center. The architectural style was reminiscent of temples of the Vijayanagara Empire. This temple was built during the time of Krishna Deva Raya. The carvings depicted tales from mythology with female figures in the classic *tribhanga* pose. Lots of flowers, birds, crocodiles and tortoise motifs were strewn around. Probably a depiction of the flora and fauna that flourished in the region.

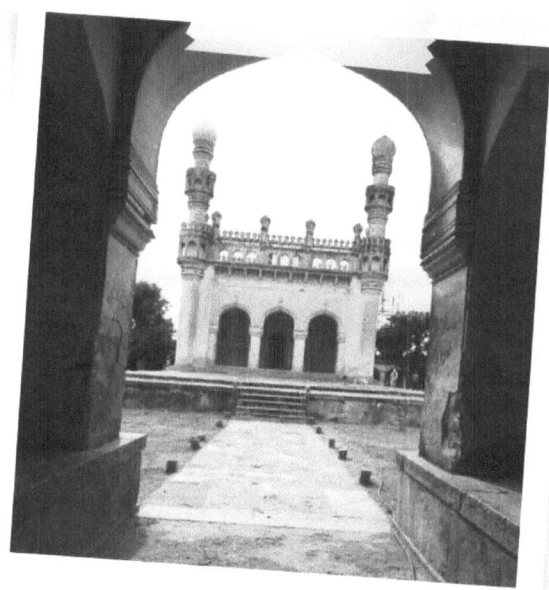

Jama Masjid framed by archway

Next up on my trail was the Jama Masjid complex. A gateway of arches ushered me inside. As soon as I walked in, I noticed that it had the same stamp of the architecture of the Qutub Shahi dynasty. I felt compelled to check out the intricate work on the minarets. Here again, I noticed delicate carvings with some remnants of color still in them. I could only imagine how beautiful they must have been centuries ago. The lotus motif showed up time and again, as it does in most Islamic carvings and paintings in India.

The prayer courtyard had a fountain in the center. It used to be supplied with water from the Pennar.

I am aware that most of these forts have amazing acoustics that even modern builders cannot replicate. The Qutub Shahi dynasty, in particular, was known for its emphasis on acoustics in forts and palaces. Who has not heard of the magical acoustics of the Golconda Fort, where a clap at the entrance can be heard several kilometers up at the pinnacle? The Iranian builders who built these had mastered echo and sound wave-travel theories.

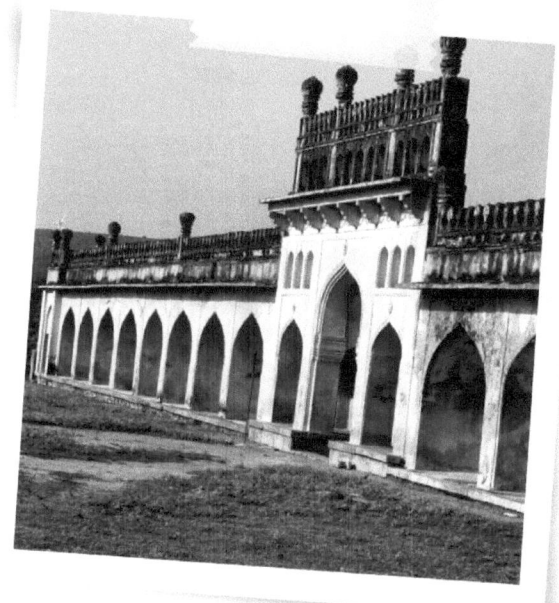

Jama Masjid entrance

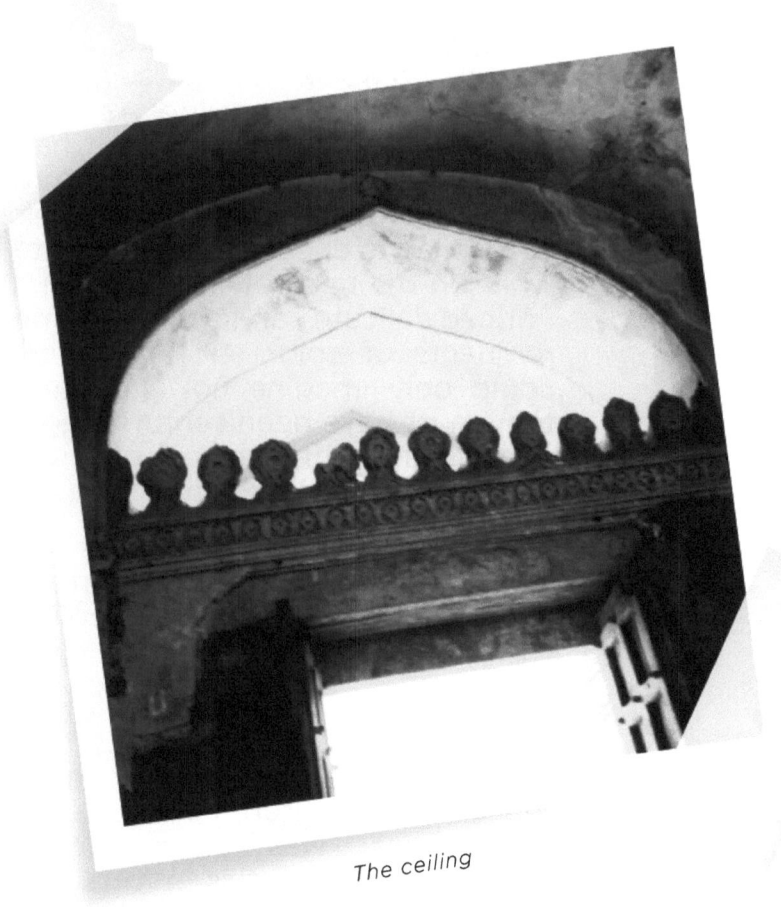

The ceiling

A note to readers: Do make it a point to look up at the ceilings, whether at the masjid or at the mandirs.

The beauty at eye level is tantalizing enough, but hidden gems can be found when you crane your neck upwards. You will be grateful that you did so, and you will undoubtedly have interesting pictures to show for it.

Beside the Jama Masjid, there was another squarish structure. It was the granary, which was used to store grains in the olden days. It functioned as a site office for the tourism board. Since I had reached the venue after government office hours, it was locked, and I missed my chance to peek inside. I hope I did not miss much.

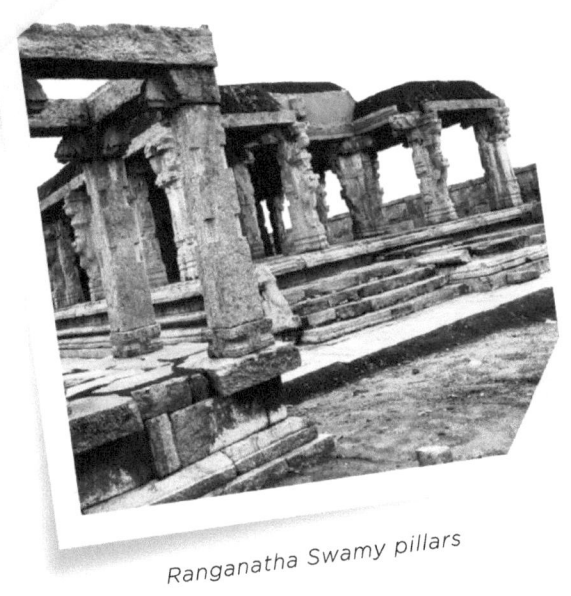

Ranganatha Swamy pillars

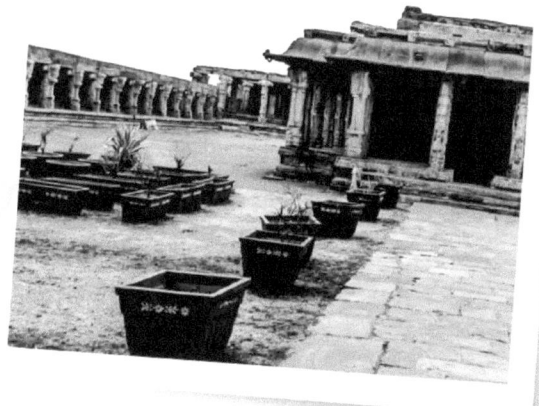

Too many potted plants

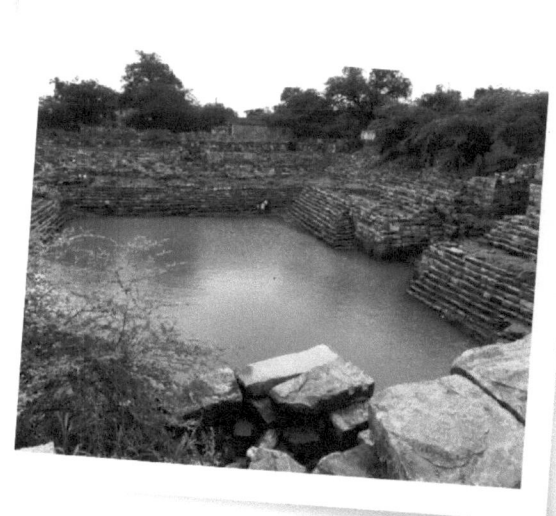

Katula Koneru

Moving on ahead, I saw the second temple in the complex, the Ranganatha Swamy Temple. It was also simpler and perhaps older. The arrangement of ruined pillars reminded me of Acropolis. Here too there was no deity in the sanctum sanctorum. Some hints of the elaborate carvings remained, like the elephants on the entrance staircase. There was an abundance of lotuses, lions and *dwarapalikas* in the *tribhanga* pose. The ceiling had carvings that had been destroyed and had weathered the wear and tear of centuries.

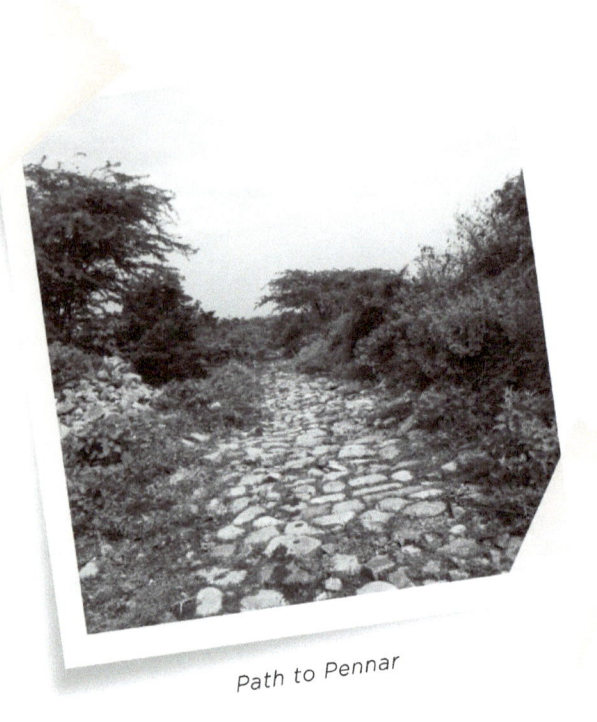

Path to Pennar

With this, I was done witnessing the man-made monuments, and it was time to keep my date with what nature had fashioned—the river and the gorge. I had saved the best for the last.

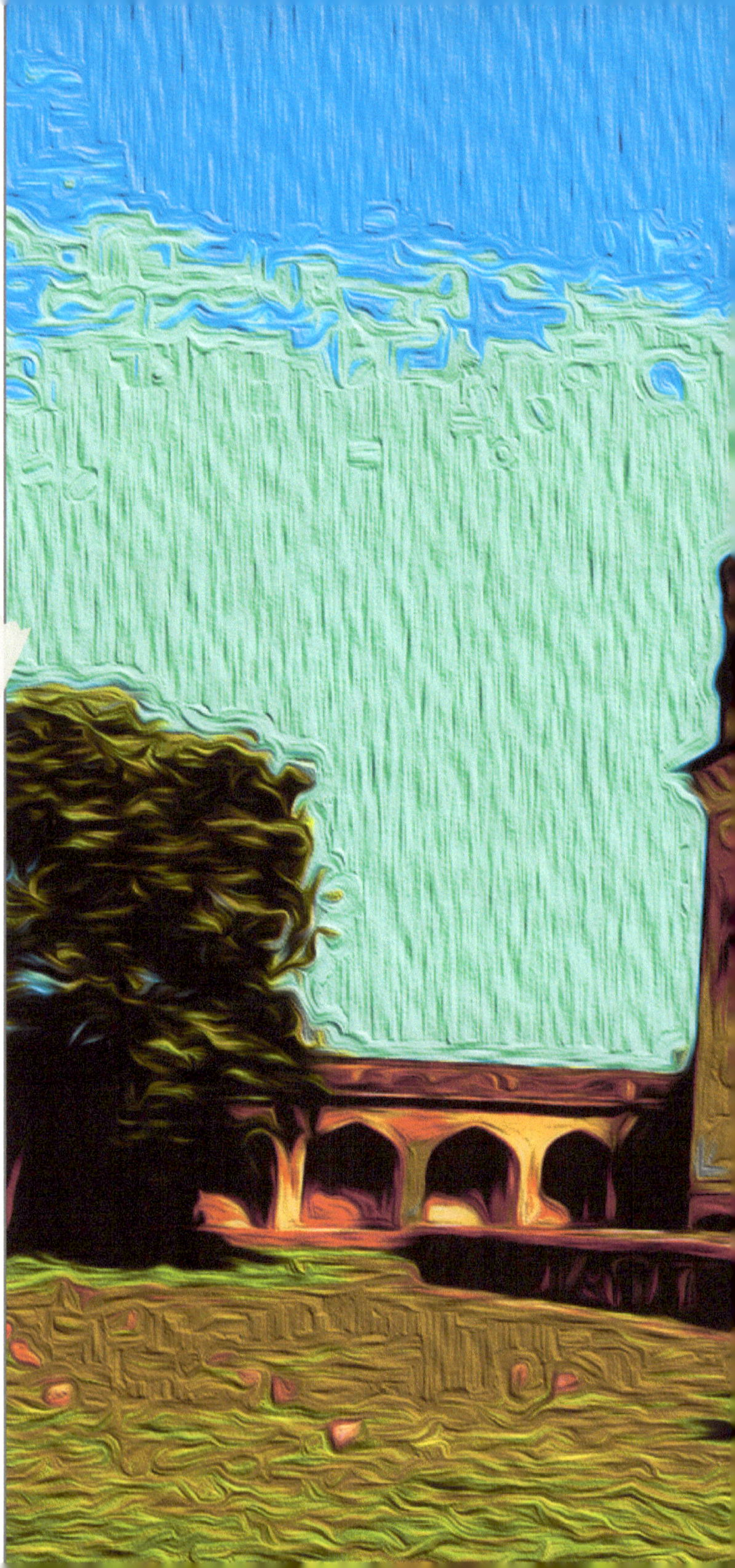

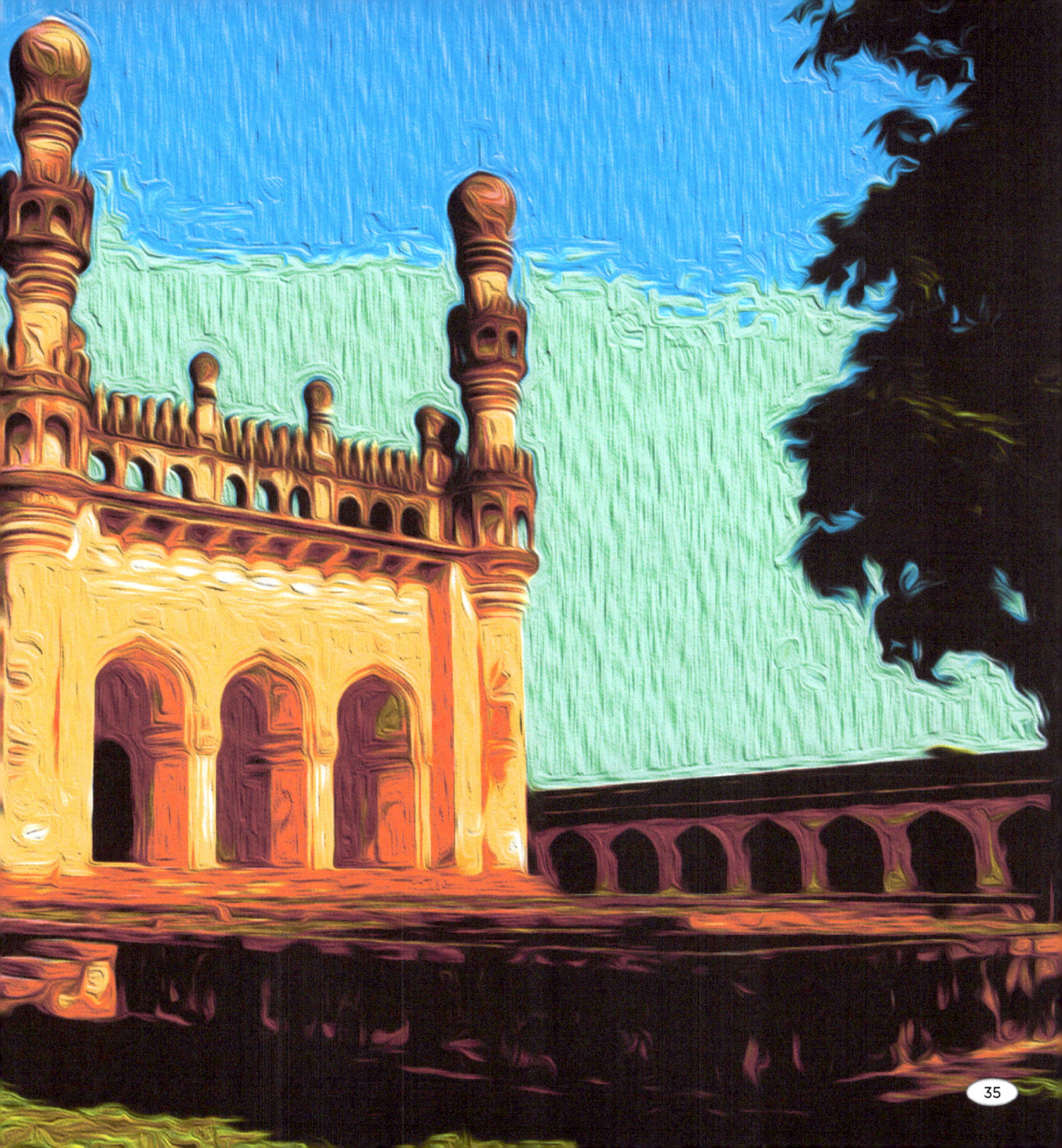

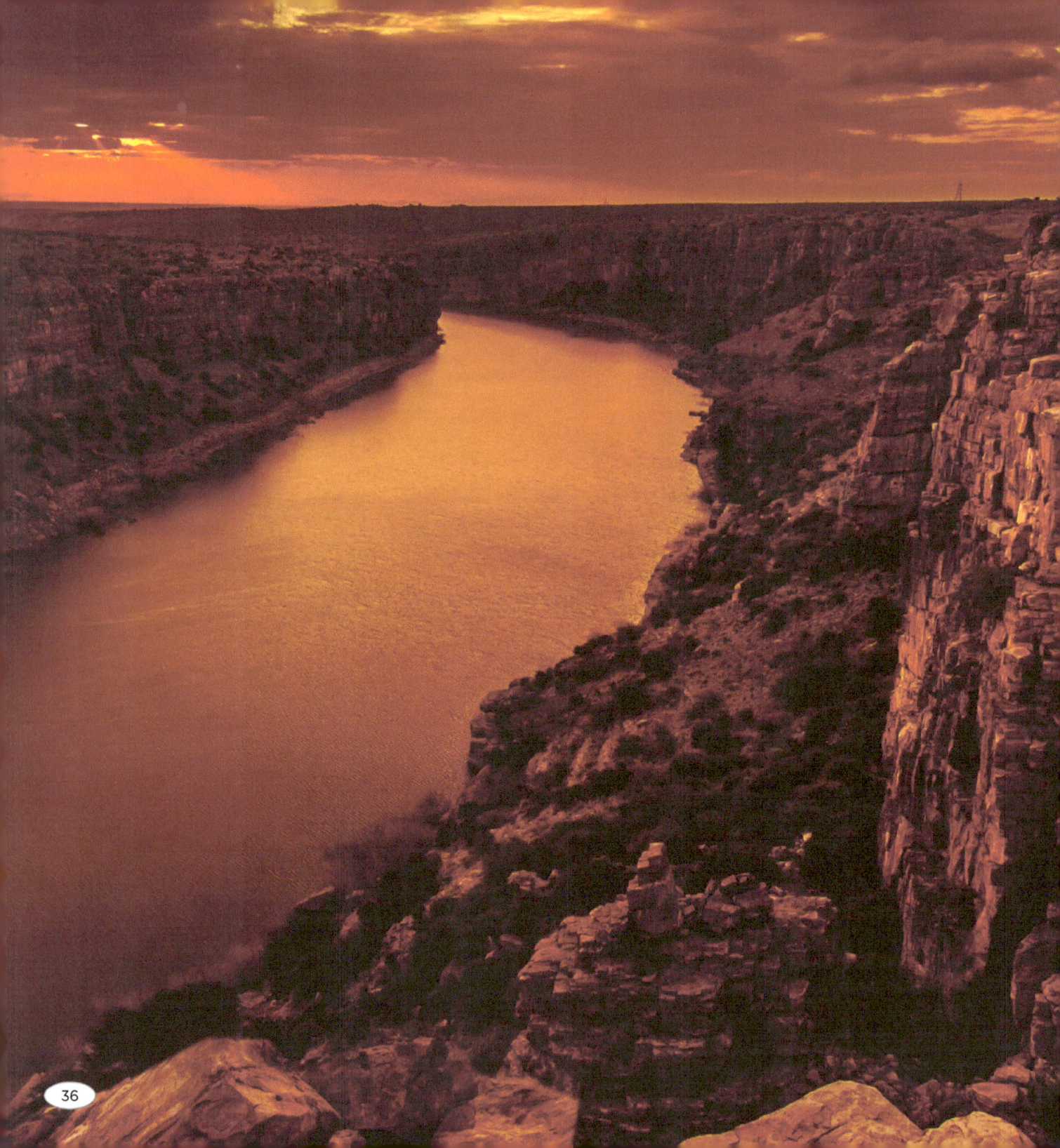

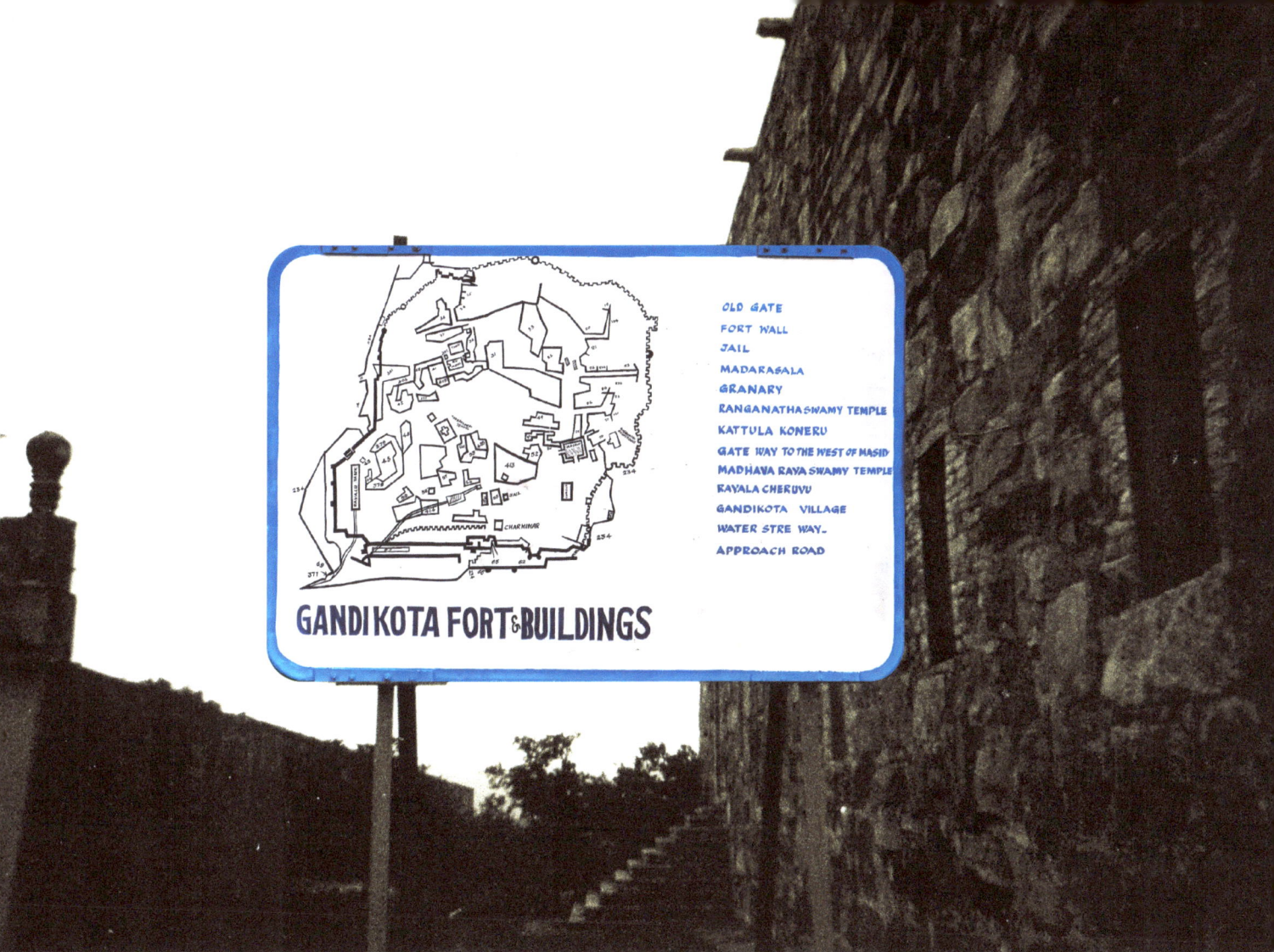

GANDIKOTA FORT & BUILDINGS

OLD GATE
FORT WALL
JAIL
MADARASALA
GRANARY
RANGANATHASWAMY TEMPLE
KATTULA KONERU
GATE WAY TO THE WEST OF MASID
MADHAVA RAYA SWAMY TEMPLE
RAYALA CHERUVU
GANDIKOTA VILLAGE
WATER STRE WAY.
APPROACH ROAD

A signboard led me in the direction of the gorge. The path was meandered, looking no different from the several trails that were strewn around the complex leading up to monuments. I held my breath to see what's on the other side— nothing, and I mean nothing I had read, seen or heard prepared me for the amazing sight that unfolded—the sheer drop of the hill range with rocks, the vista and the river below.

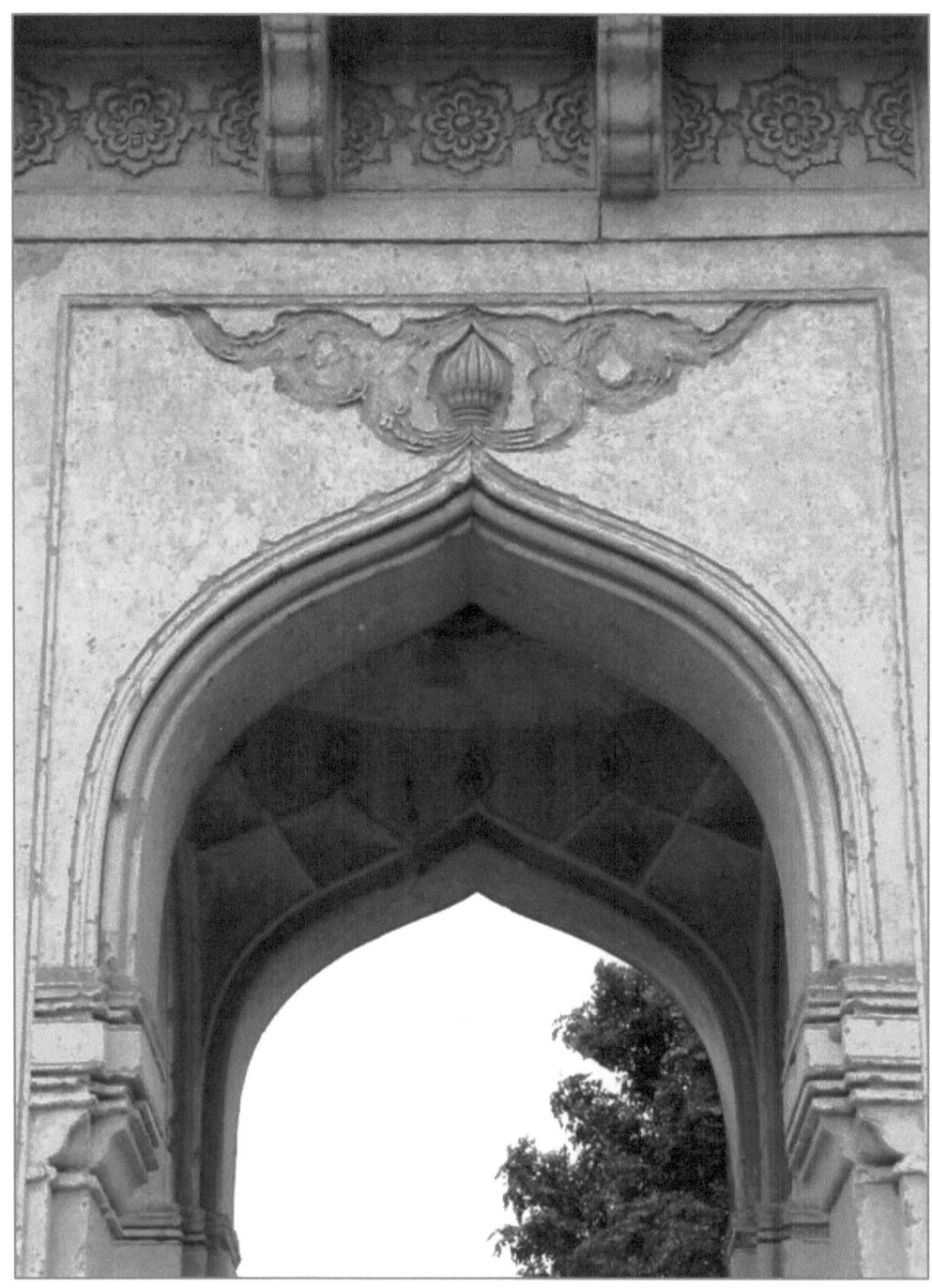

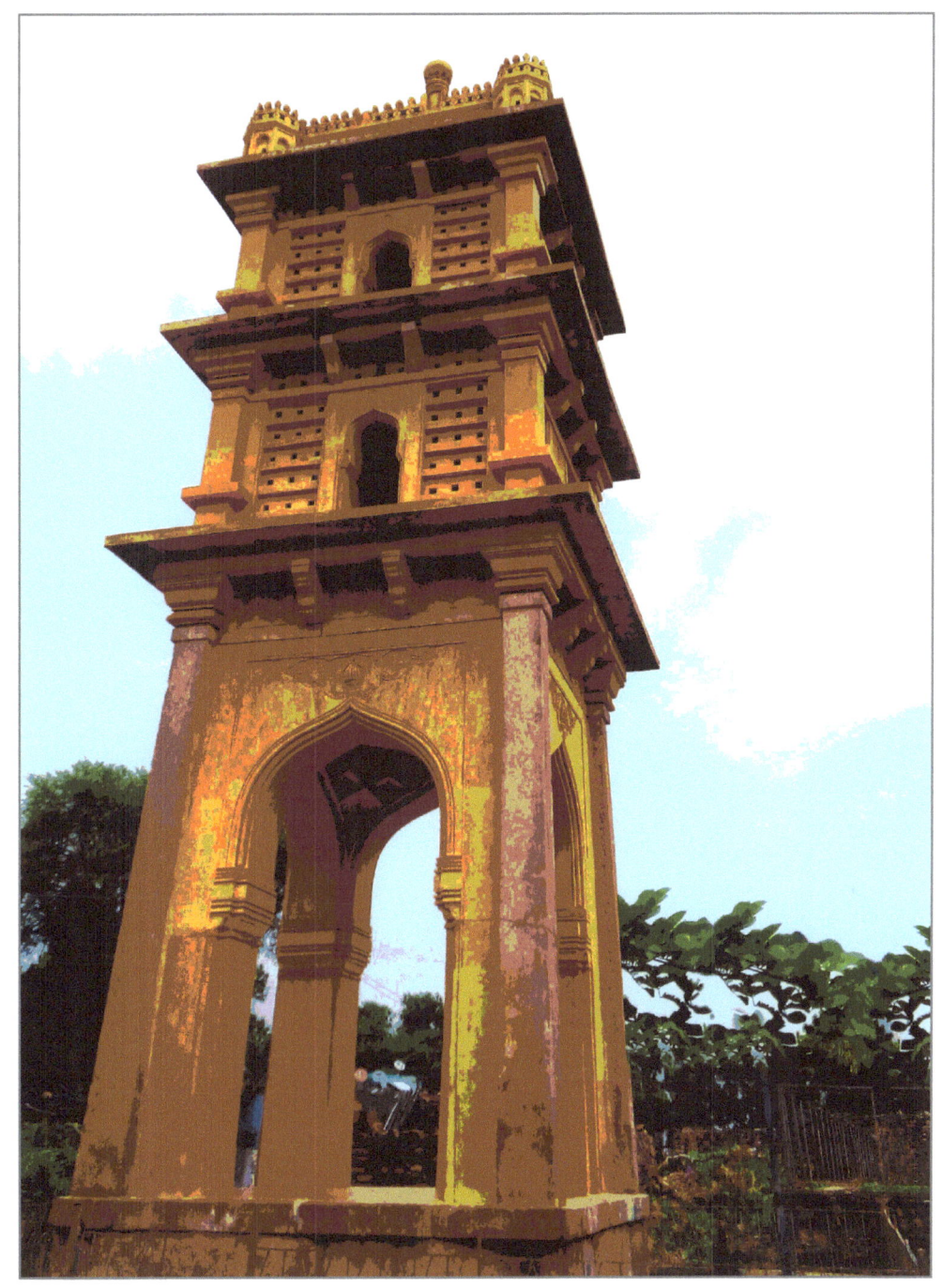

It was the highlight of my day. I thanked my stars for having started the journey disastrously, with delays, because it had ensured that I caught the sunset over Gandikota Canyon.

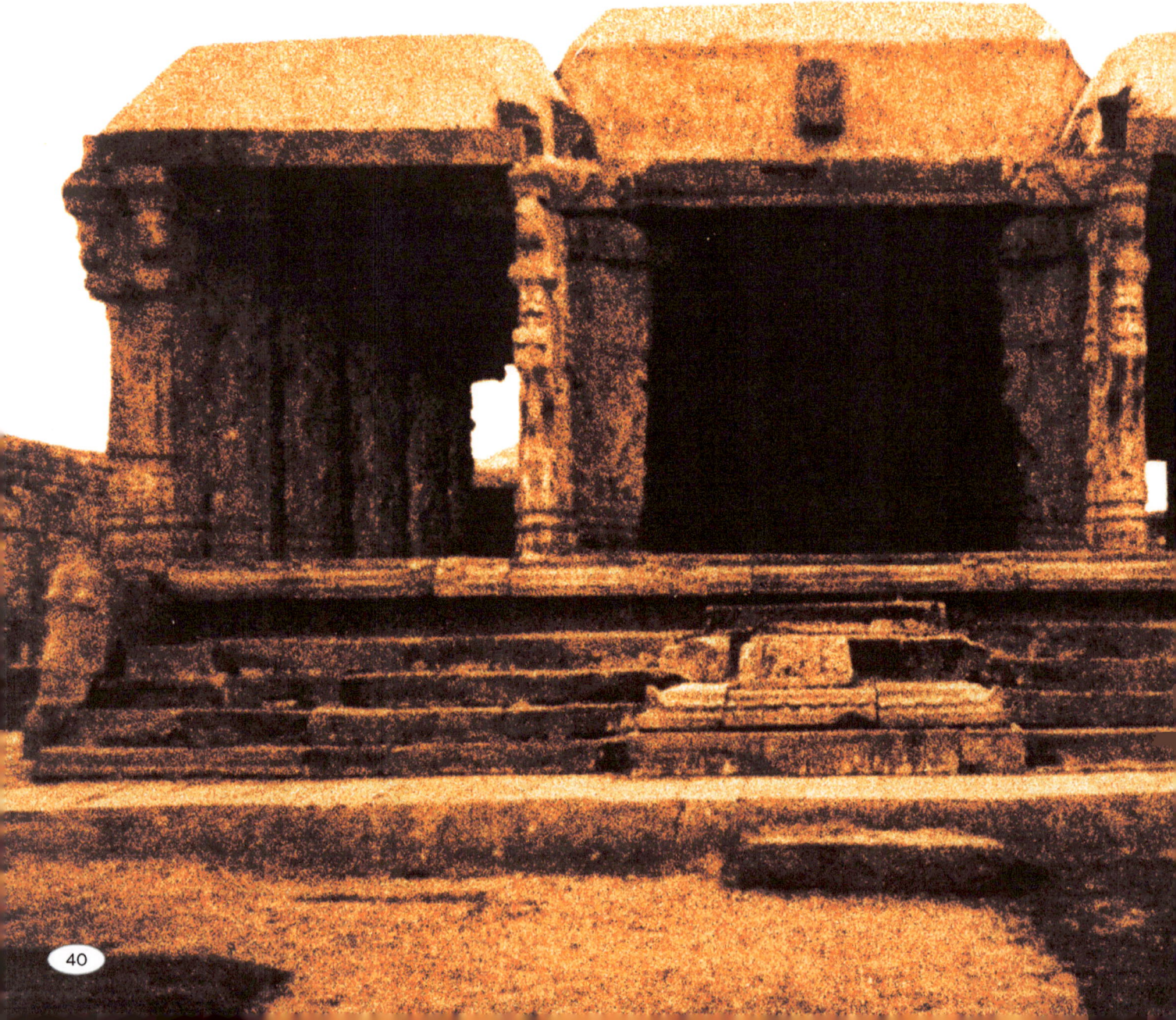

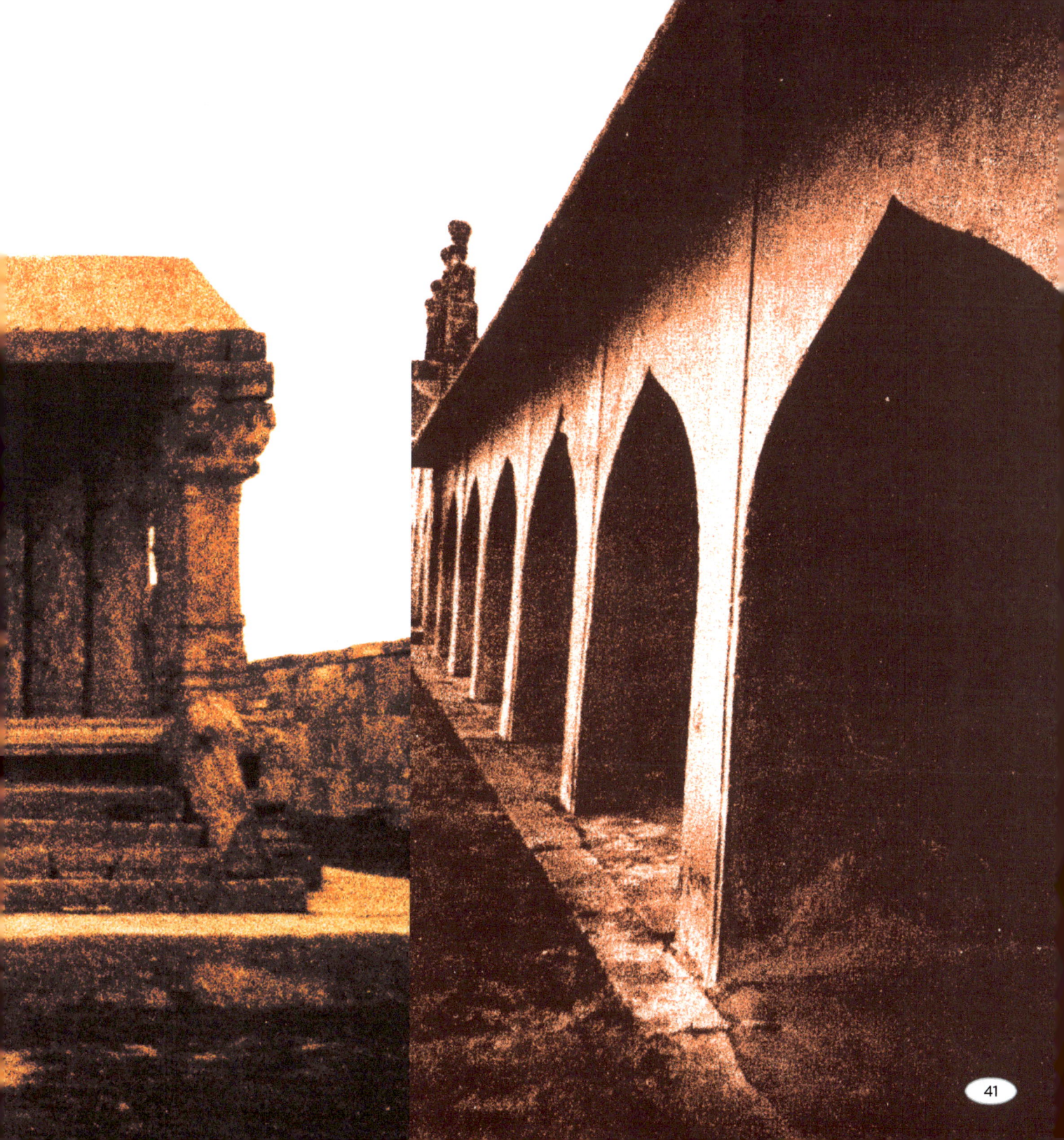

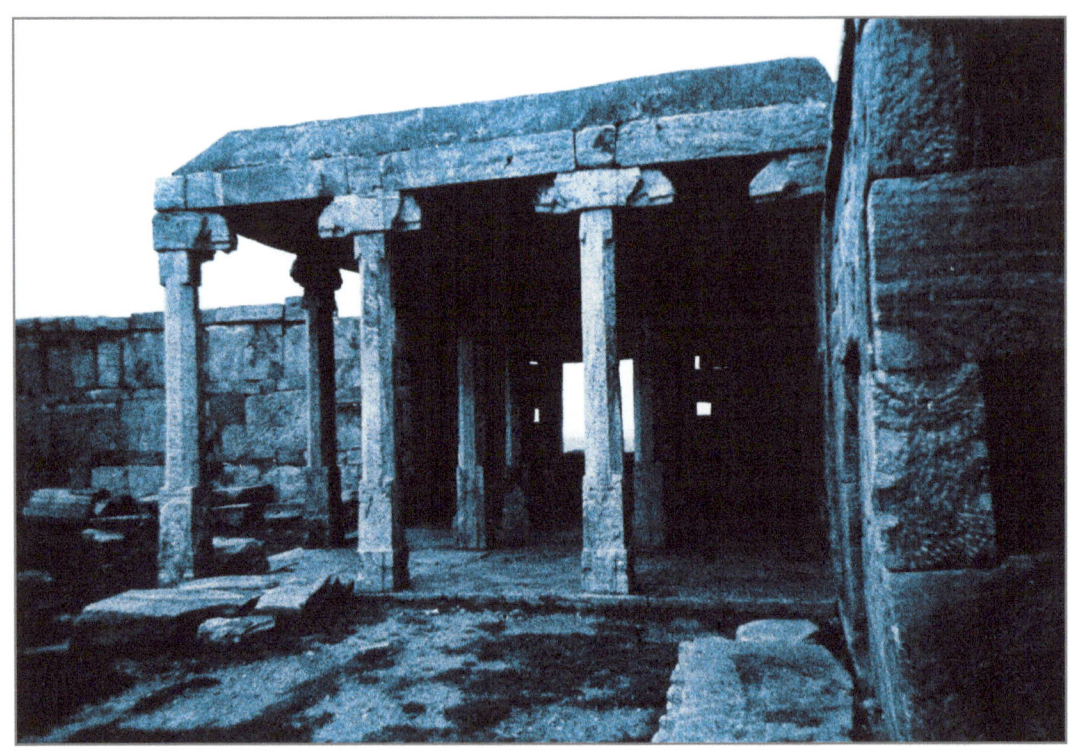

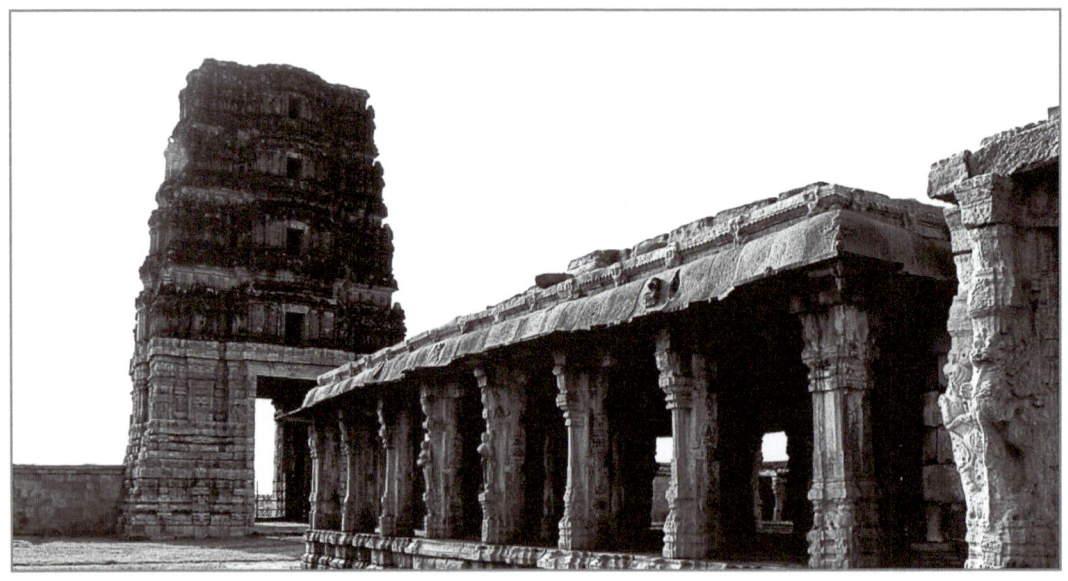

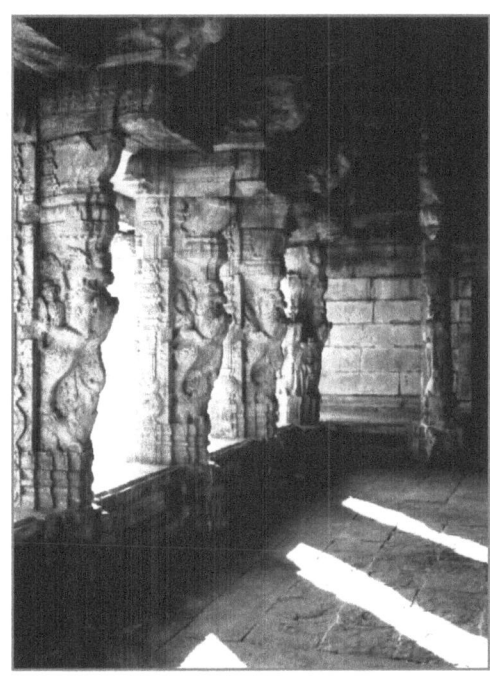

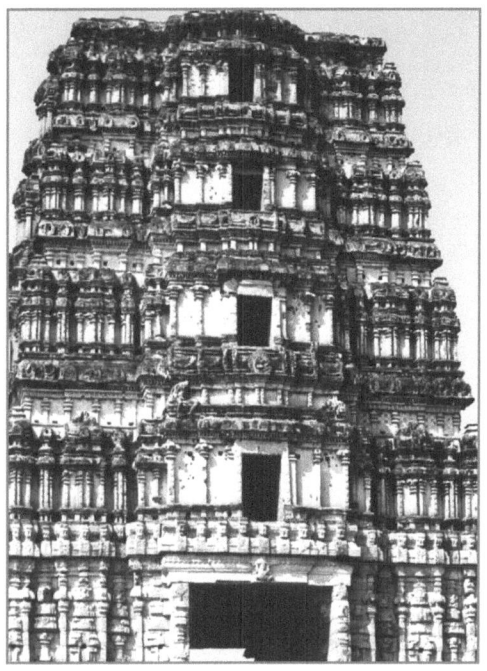

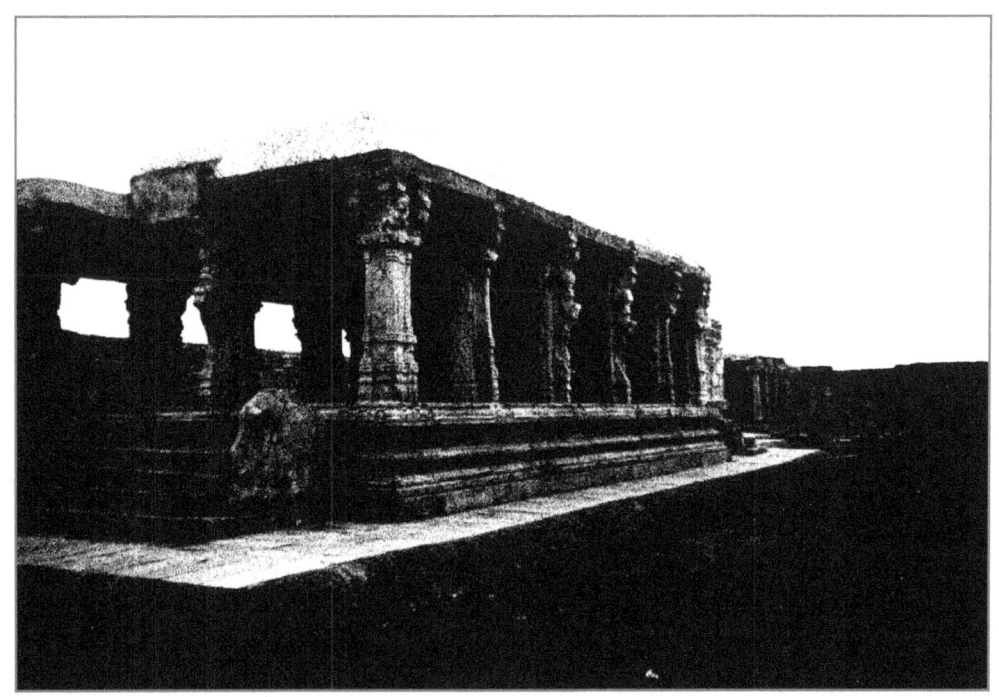

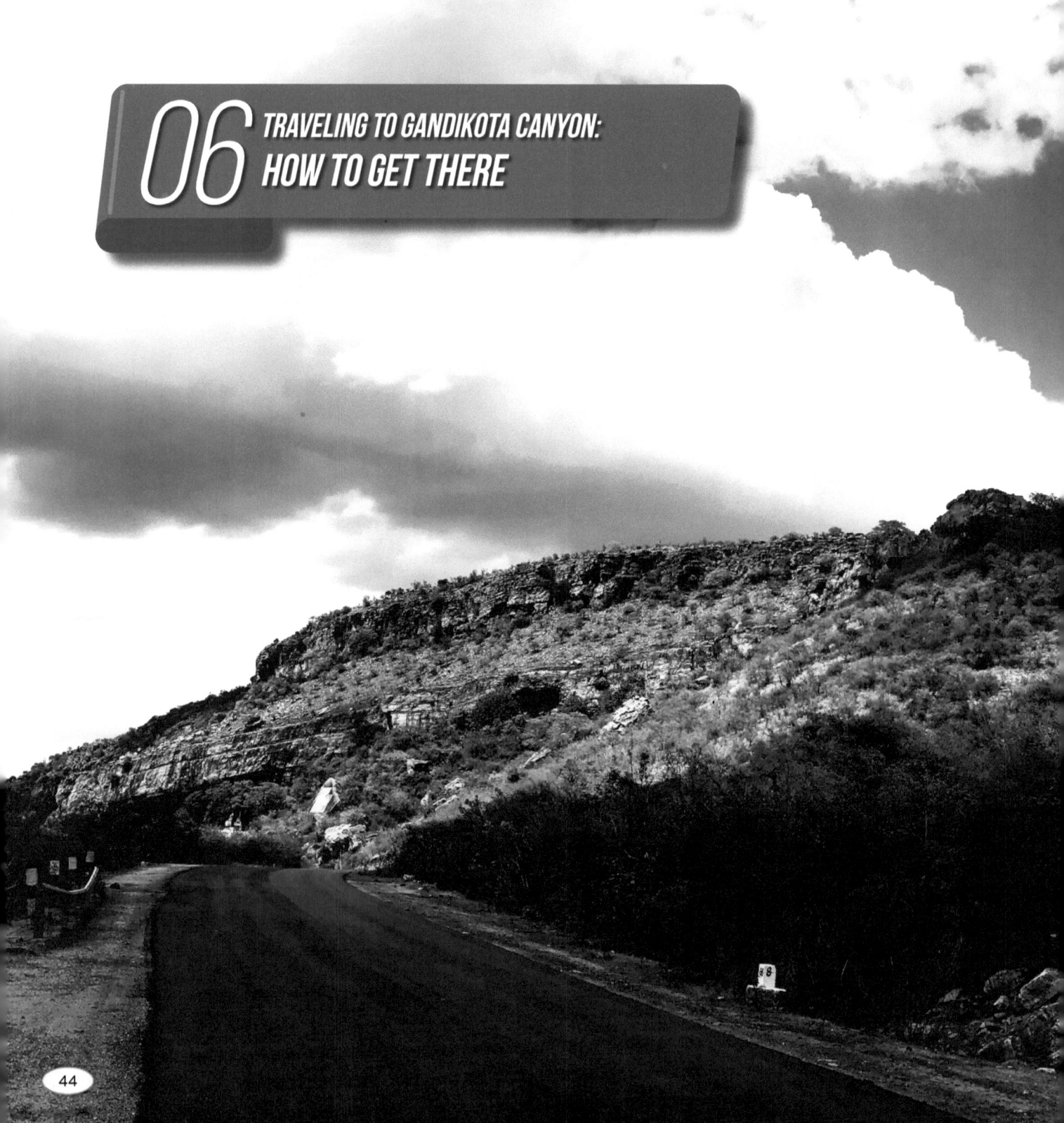

06 TRAVELING TO GANDIKOTA CANYON:
HOW TO GET THERE

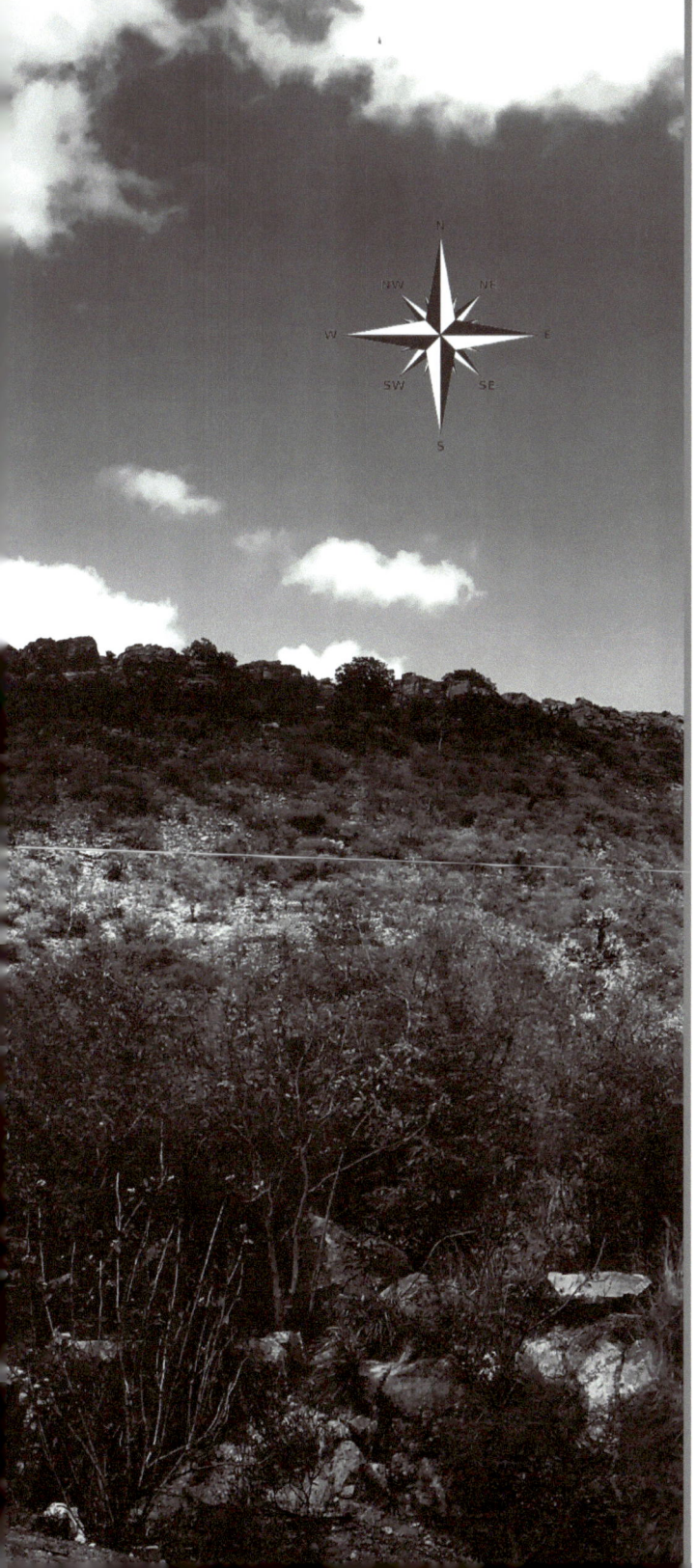

Due to the efforts of the Andhra Pradesh Tourism Development Corporation (APTDC), Gandikota is very well-connected to most of India by air, road and train. It is also heavily promoted as an unusual tourist destination, offering adventure sports like rock-climbing, rappelling, dirt-biking, off-roading, camping, canoeing and walking tours. So, plan out what you wish to do beforehand. Not to mention the freshly laid roads from the nearby town to the fort/canyon.

How to get to Gandikota

• Gandikota is approx. 281 km from Bengaluru, 362 km from Hyderabad, 398 km from Vijayawada and 226 km from Tirupati.

• Hire a private taxi, or go on a road trip in your own car. There's ample parking space in the complex.

• Jammalamdugu is the closest town to Gandikota being 16 km away. Muddanur is 25 km away, Proddutur is 40 km away, and Tadipathri is 80 km away. Autos are available from Jammalamdugu.

• From Hyderabad city, it took me eight hours in a private taxi (due to the delay caused by rain, otherwise seven hours is what you can expect).

- It takes four-and-a-half hours by road from Bengaluru.

- The closest airports are Tirupati and Bengaluru.

- The nearest railway station is Muddanuru (Hyderabad-Tirupati Line).

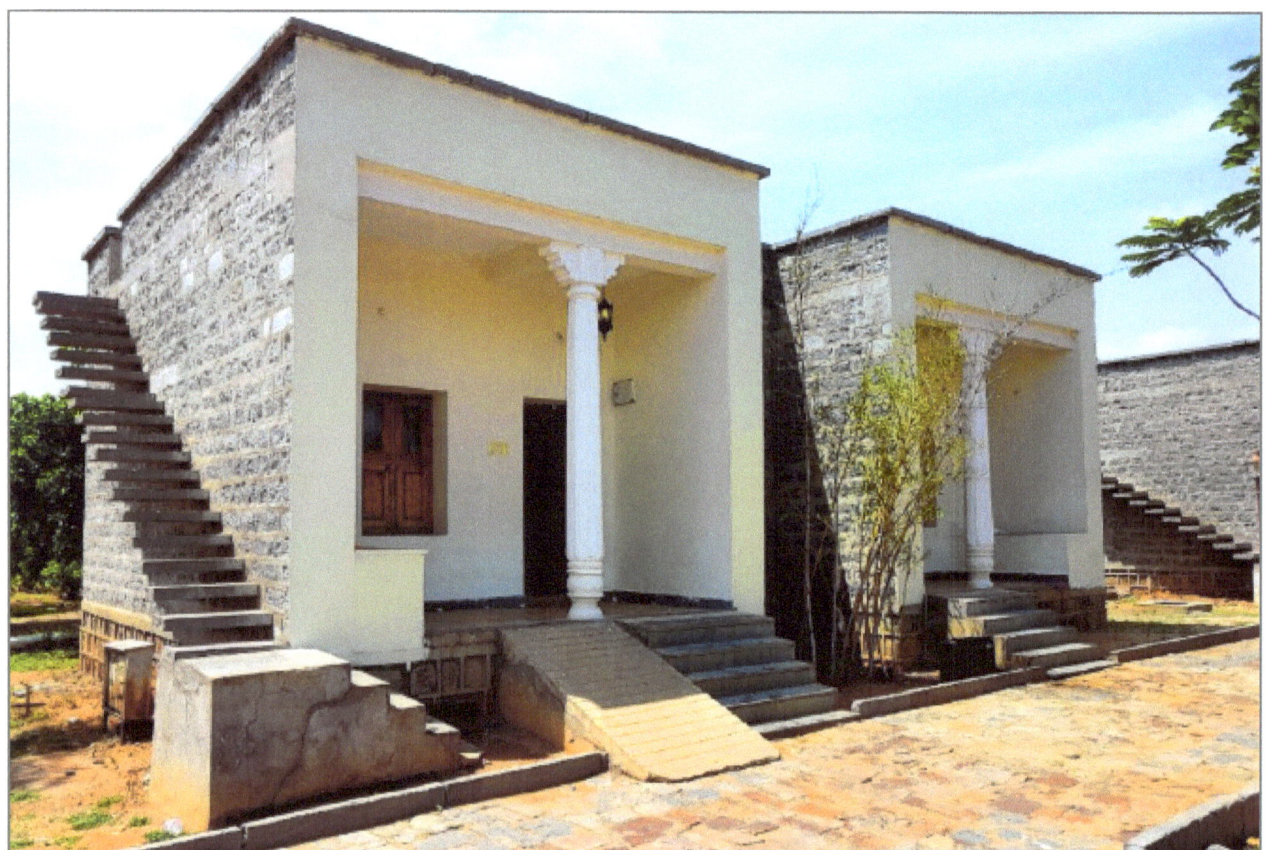

Where to Stay

- An overnight trip is recommended, as the fort is open 24 hours. You can catch the sunrise and/ or the sunset—both spectacular sights.

- At Gandikota, there is just the AP tourism corporation's Haritha Resort. Its proximity of only 500 meters from the fort makes it a prime location. The tariff is reasonable, usually Rs. 1500 per day on weekdays, going up to Rs. 2000 per day for an AC room. Dormitory rooms and non-AC rooms are also available. Book in advance during peak season. Since most people stay overnight only, it's made worthwhile by the gorge. They have a limited food menu.

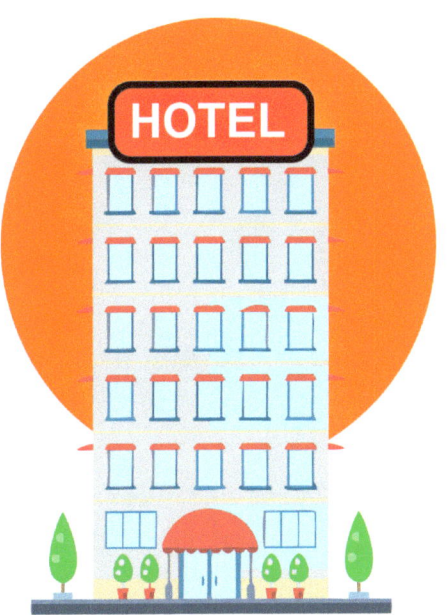

Haritha Hotel

http://aptdc.gov.in

1800-42-545454

Gandikota Road, Gandikota,
Andhra Pradesh – 516 434

(big parking area at the hotel)

- There are many excellent hotels in Jammalamduggu and Proddutur if you cannot get a booking in Haritha. Definitely try them out, especially if you have your own vehicle.

• BGR Residency

Sundaracharyula St., Sarvakatta,
Proddatur, Andhra Pradesh
Ph: 091776 64963

For adventure-sport junkies, there are plenty of options available in Gandikota, from kayaking, rappelling, biking, rock-climbing to night-camping under the stars.

Some of the rocks are loose and have caused many an accident. If you plan to camp overnight under the stars, tents are available with AP-Tourism-approved operators as well as private operators. There are enough public toilets in the Gandikota Fort complex.

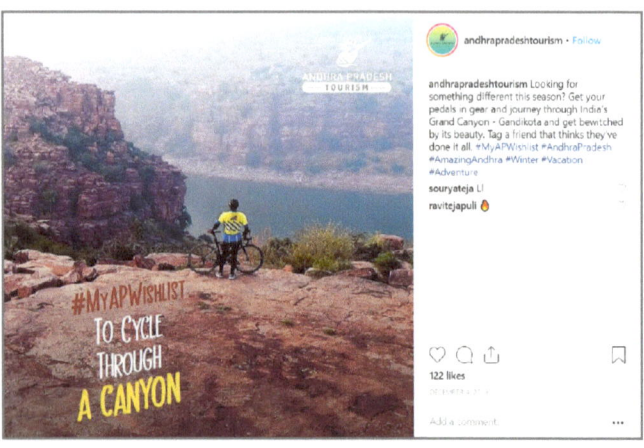

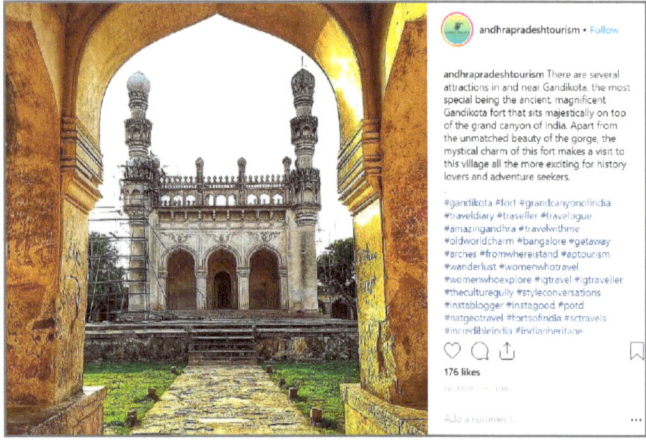

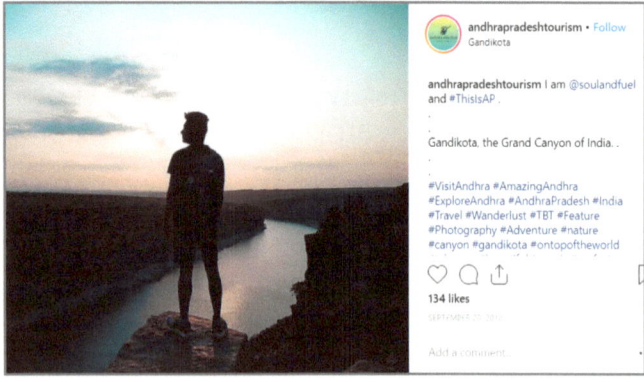

#andhrapradeshtourism

All images screen grabbed from the AP tourism Instagram page for purpose of explanation. Do follow their page for updates on events and thrilling pictures. Also a good way to connect with fellow tourists

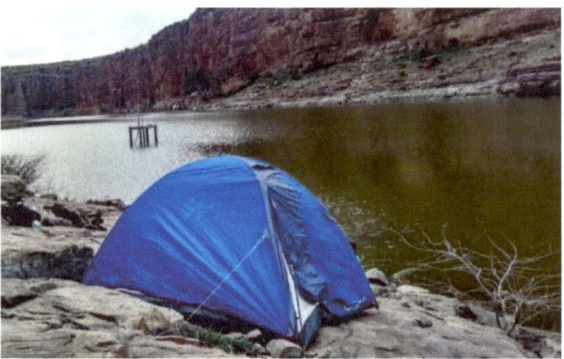

Some of the popular private adventure tour operators can be found on Thrillophilia and BookMyShow. Check their websites for more information and online booking.

https://www.thrillophilia.com/tours/gandikota-camping-and-trekking-experience

www.bookmyshow.com

Camping experience can be had with Gandikota Adventure Club and Gandikota Tourism Campsite.

Both these are at the venue; you can enroll yourself for a night stay when you arrive.

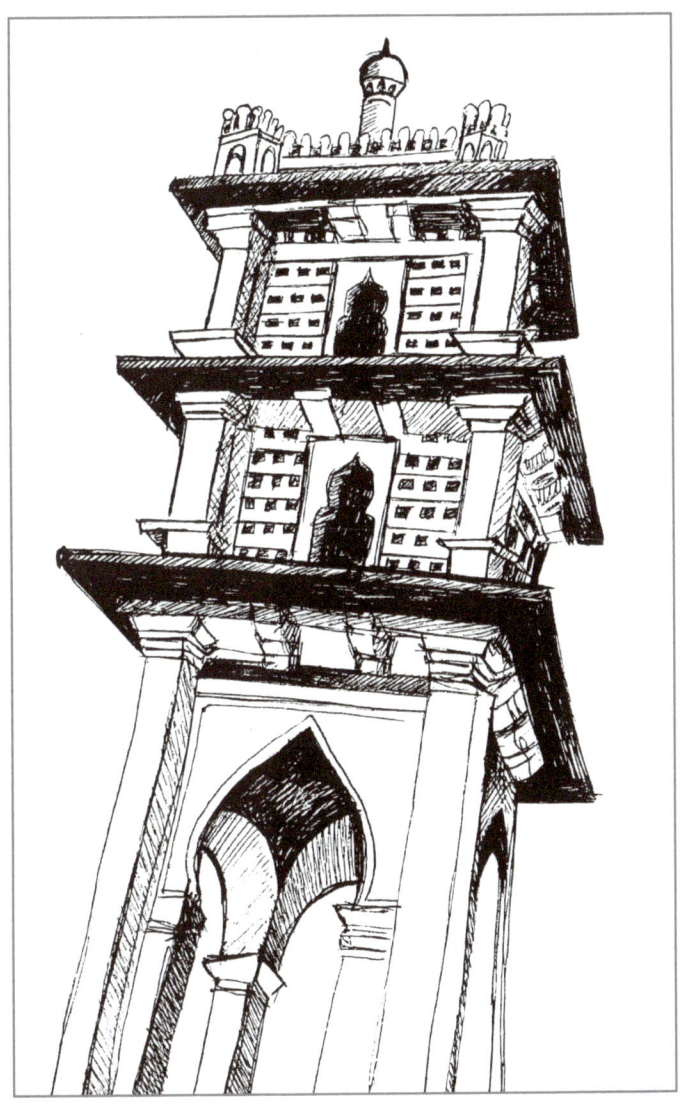

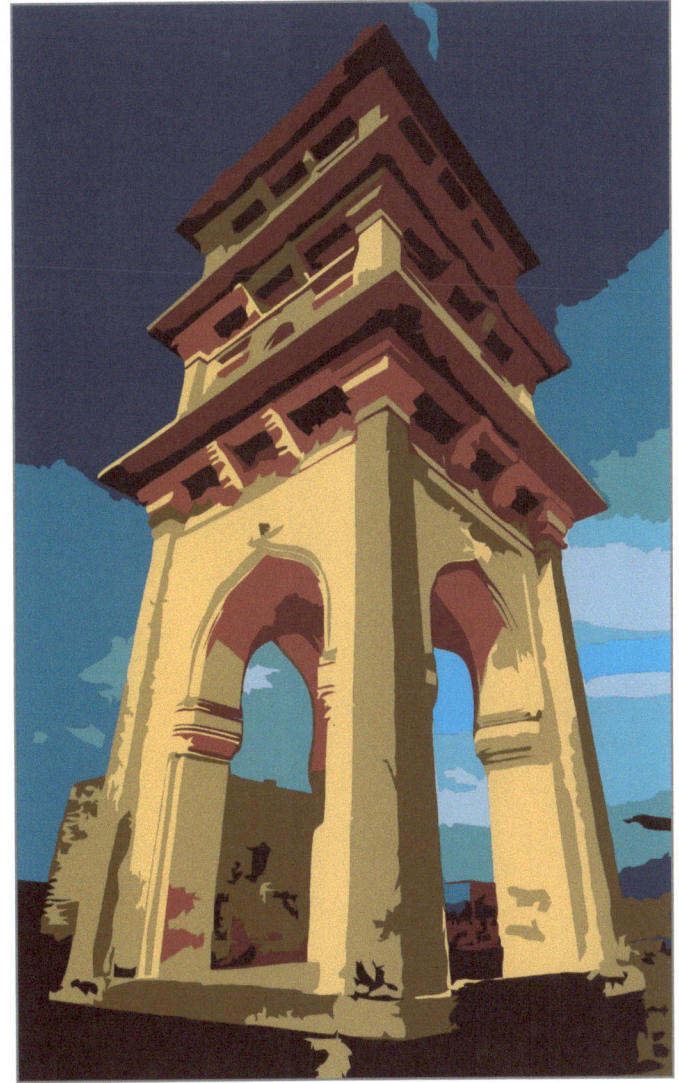

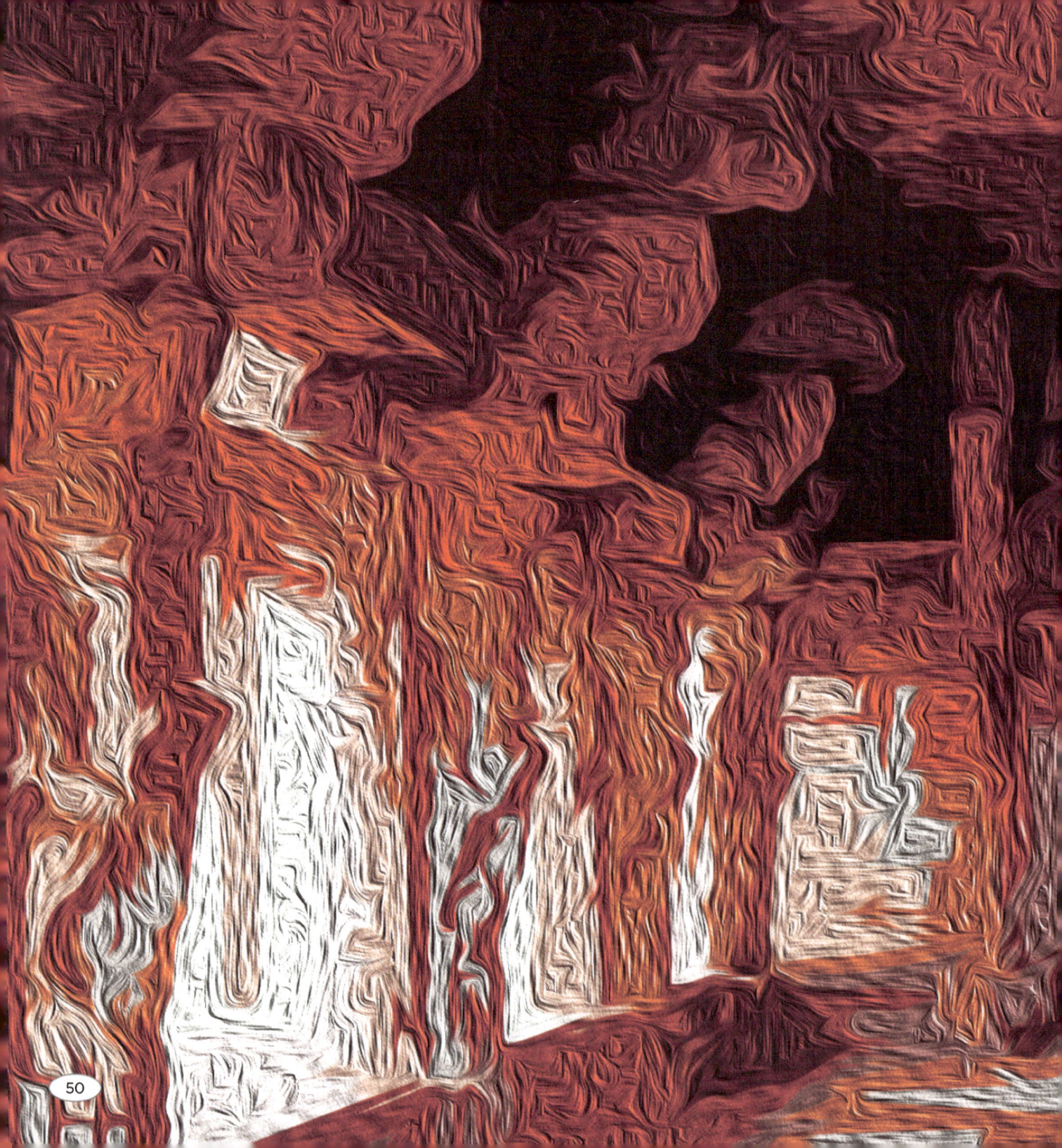

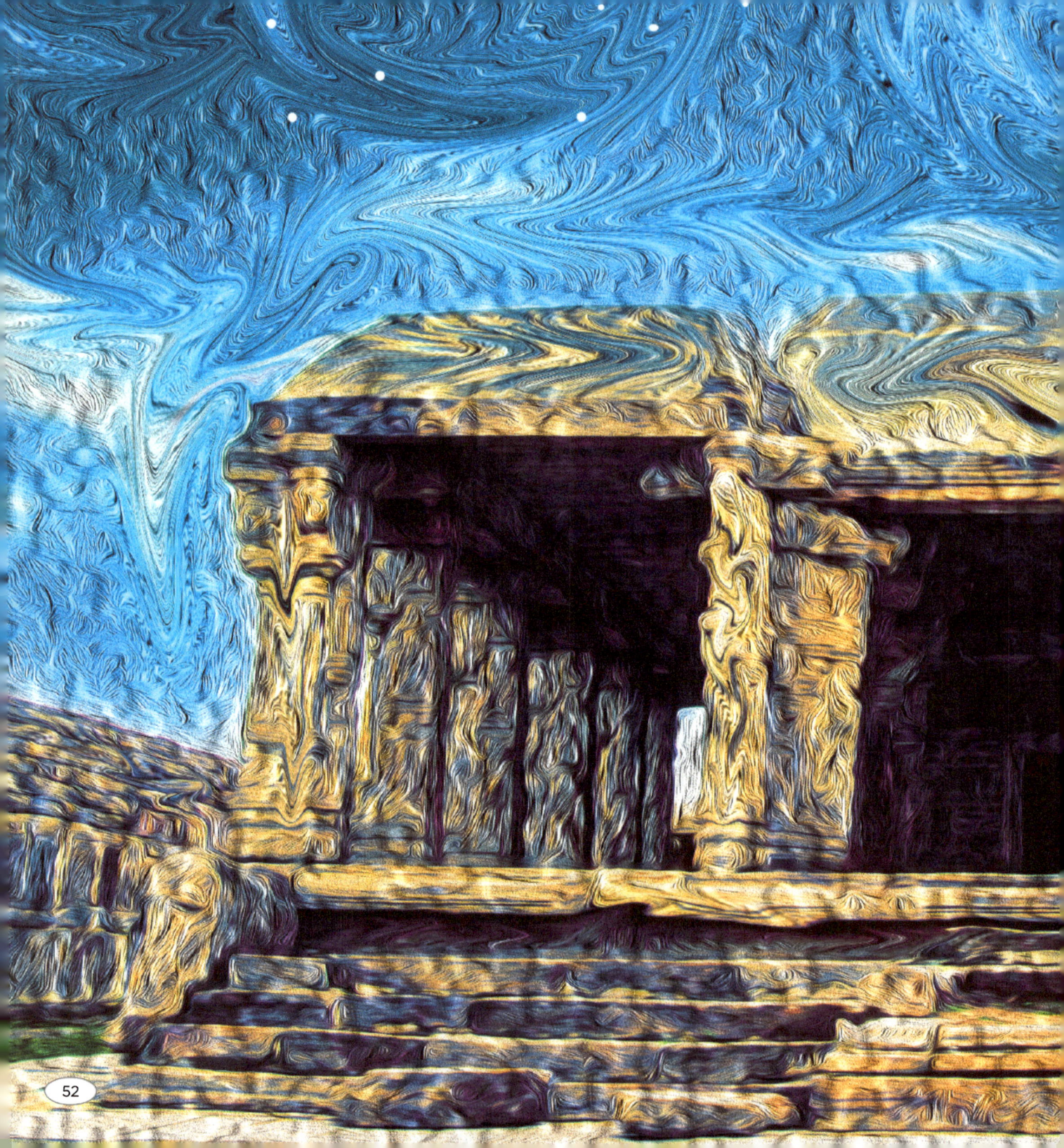

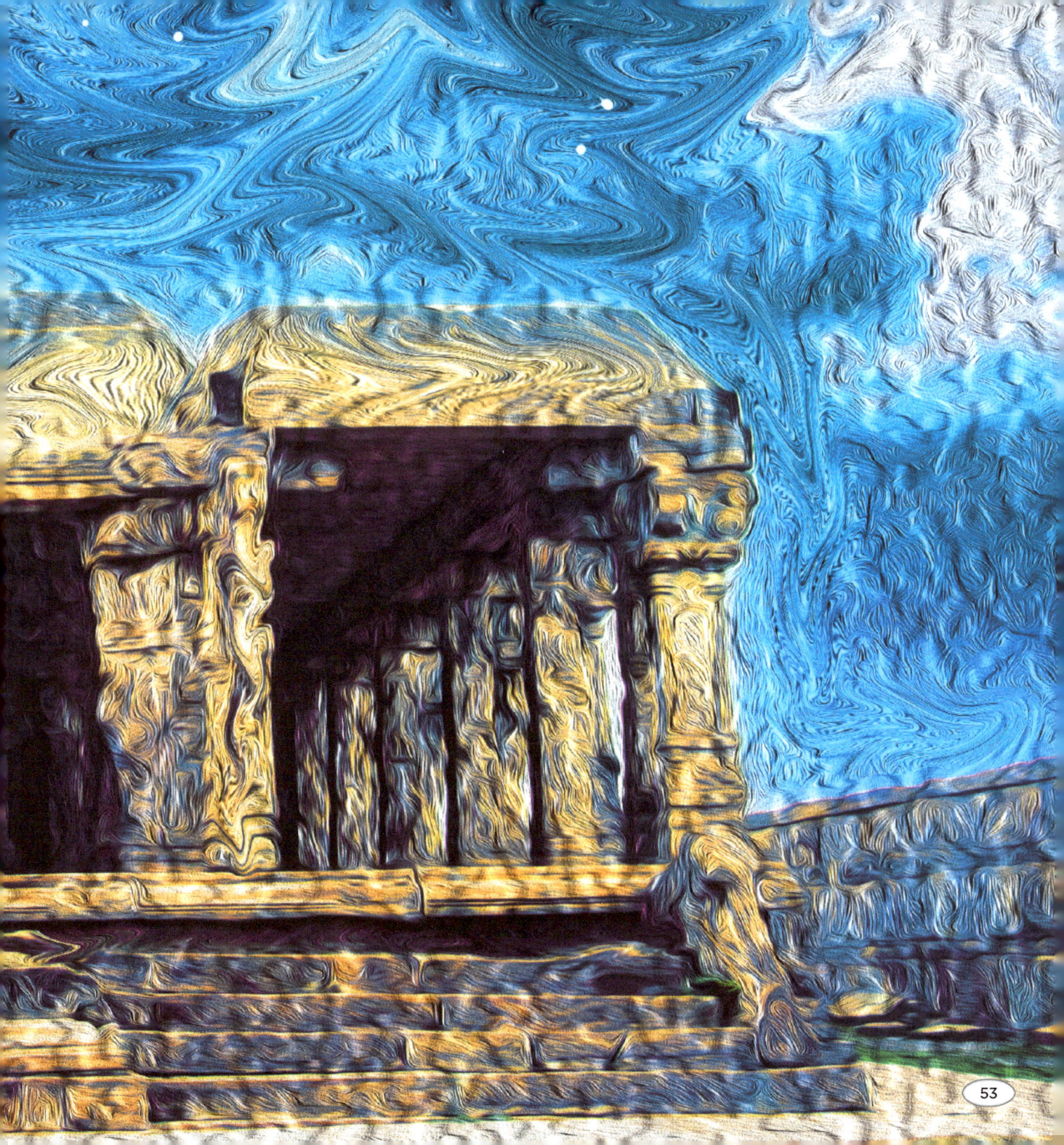

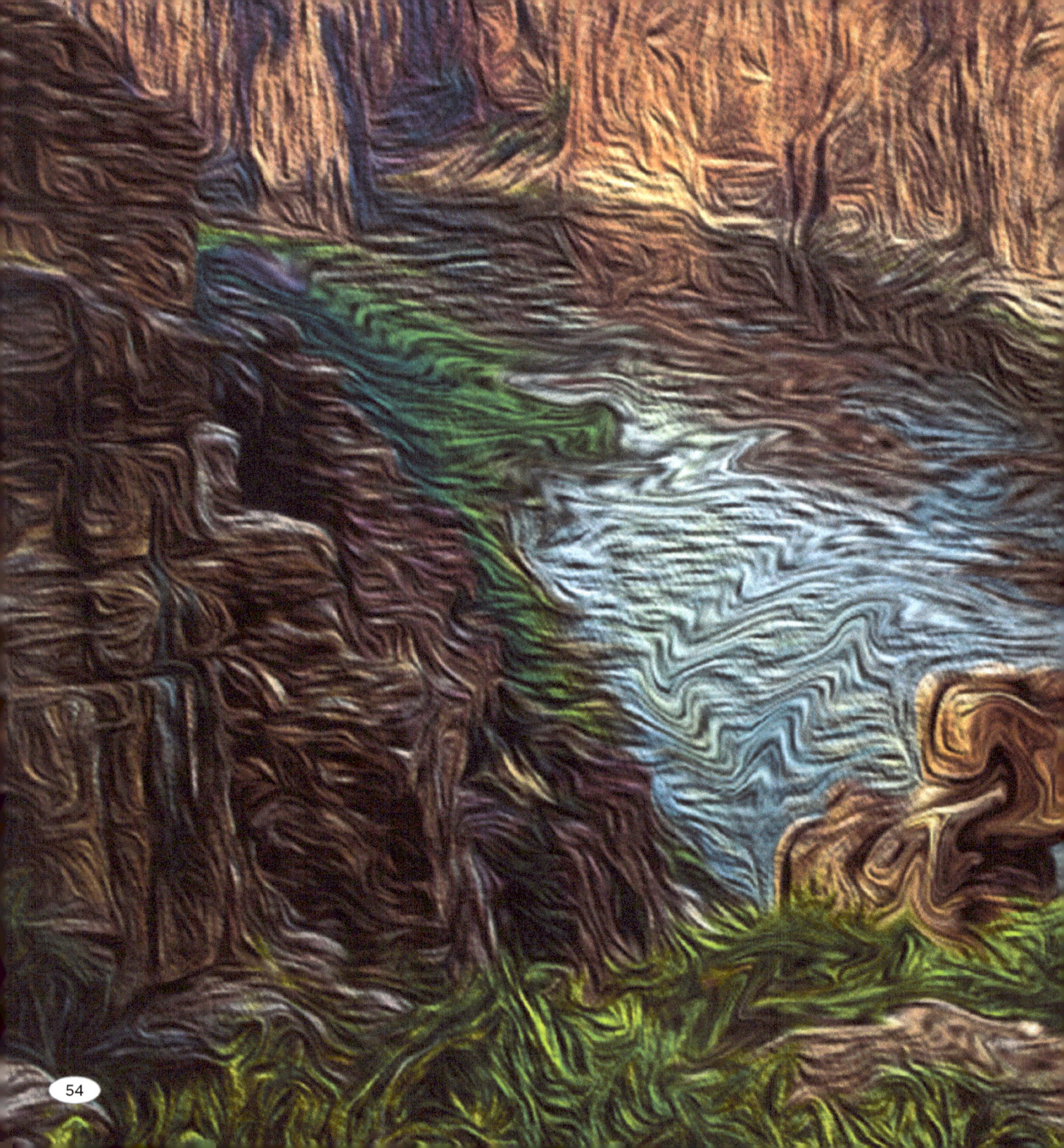

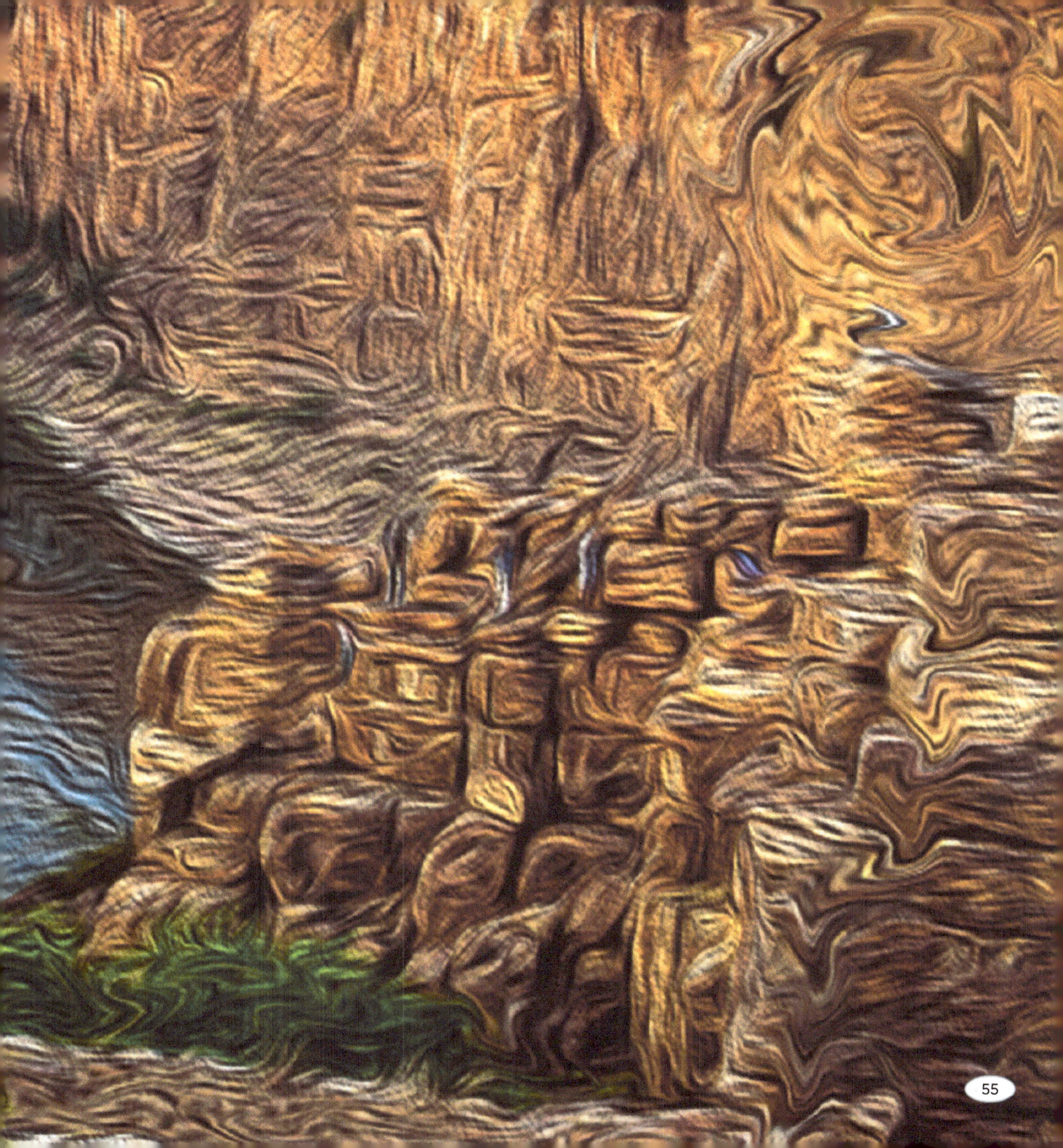

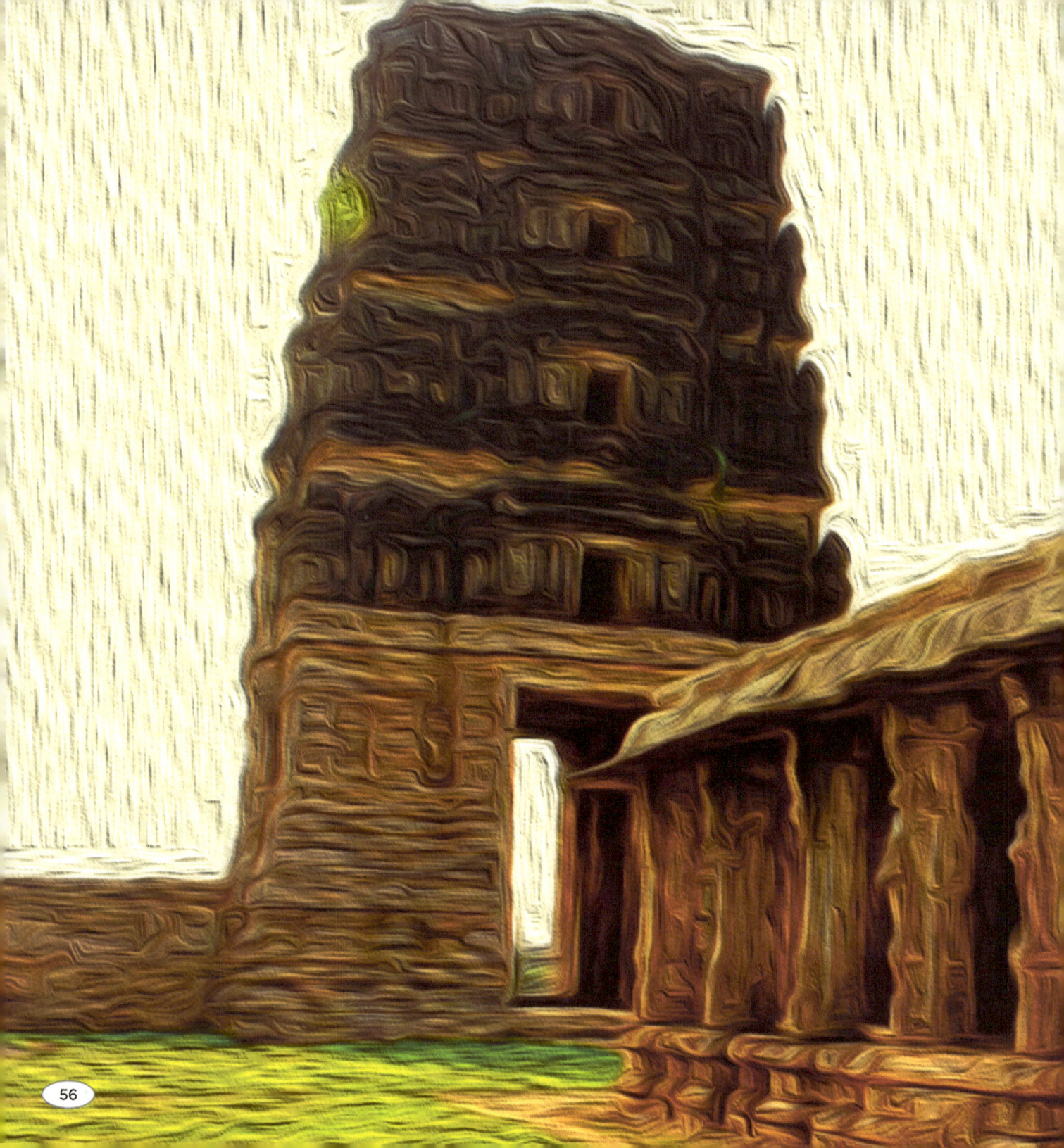

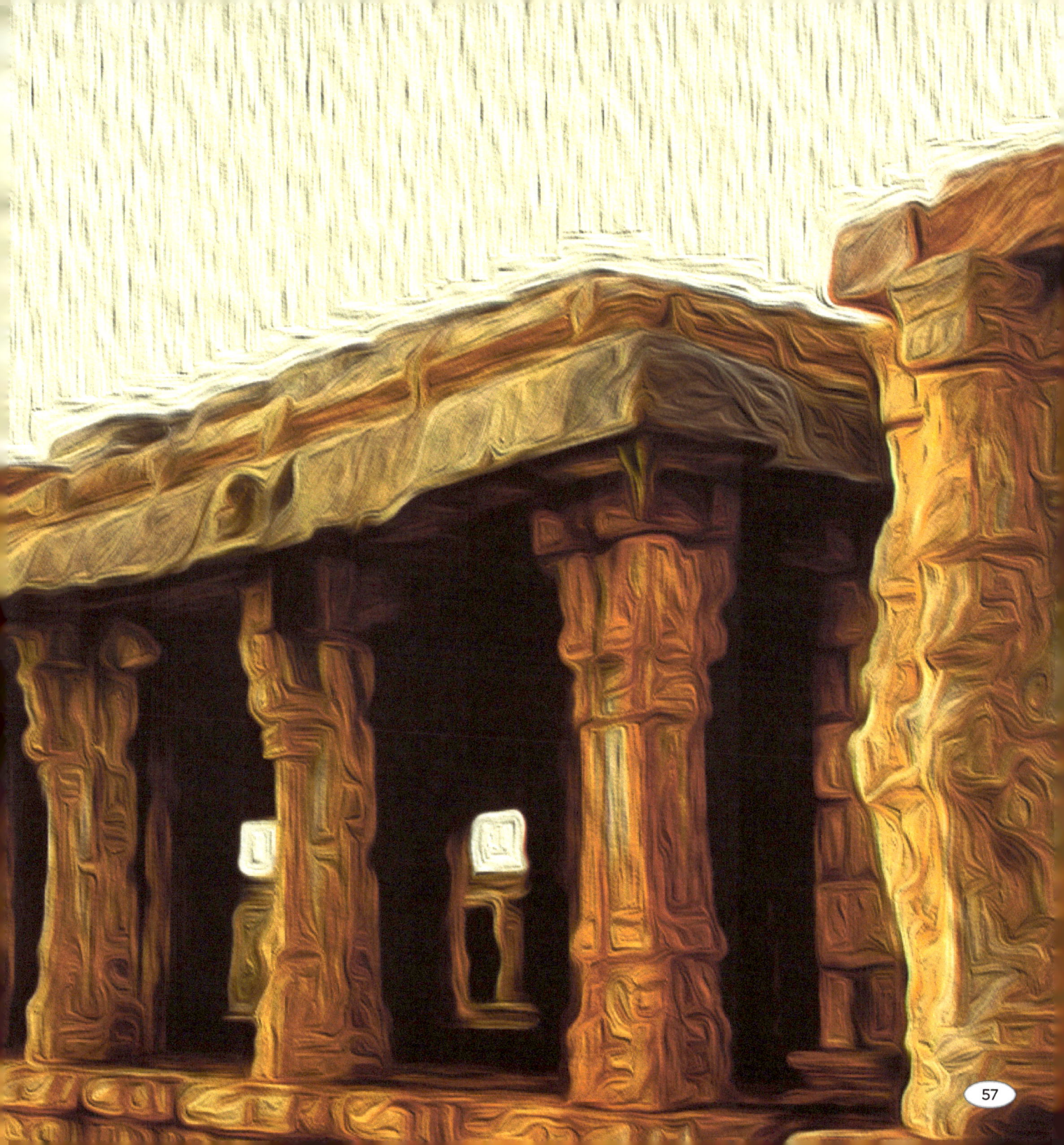

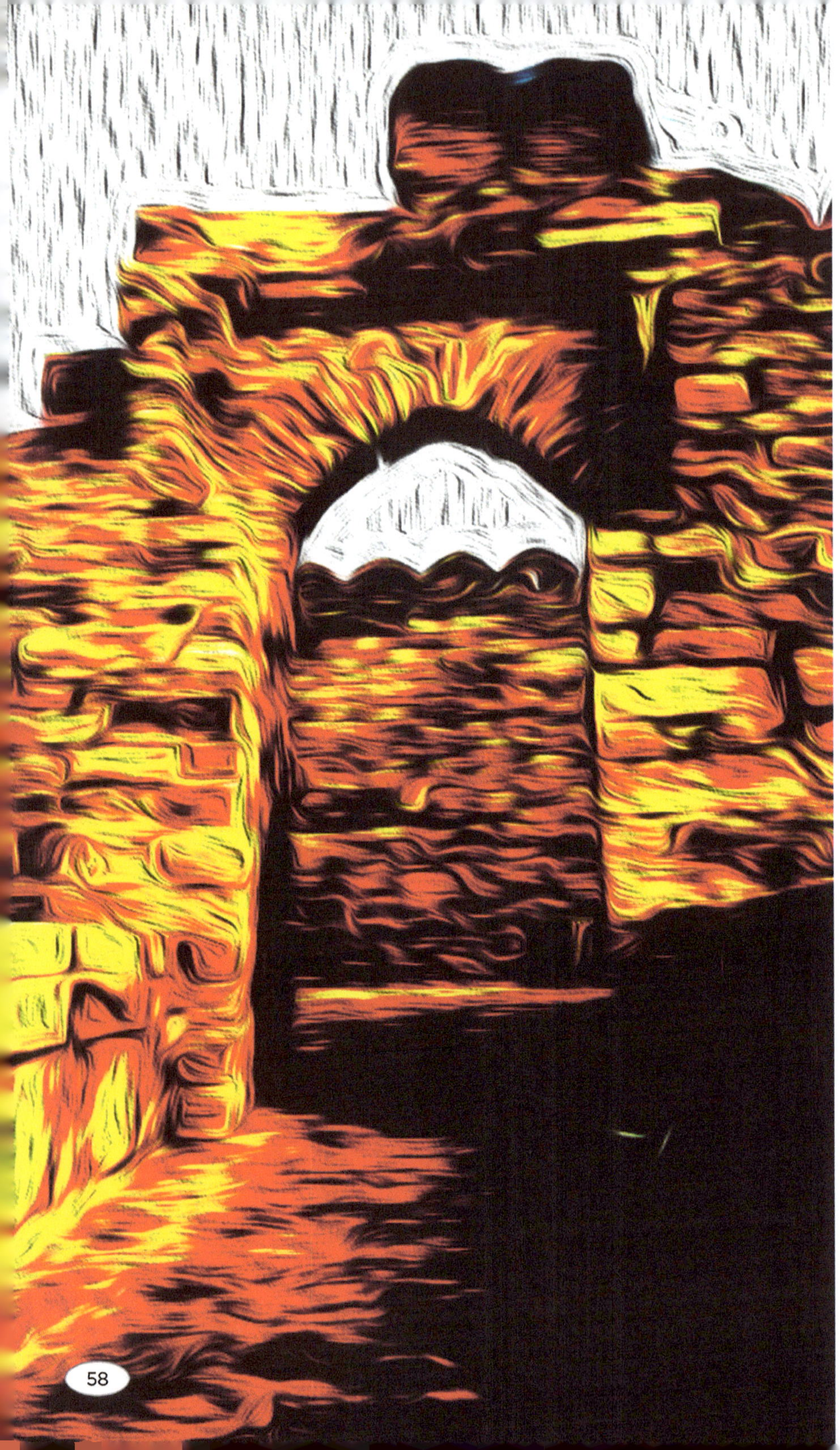

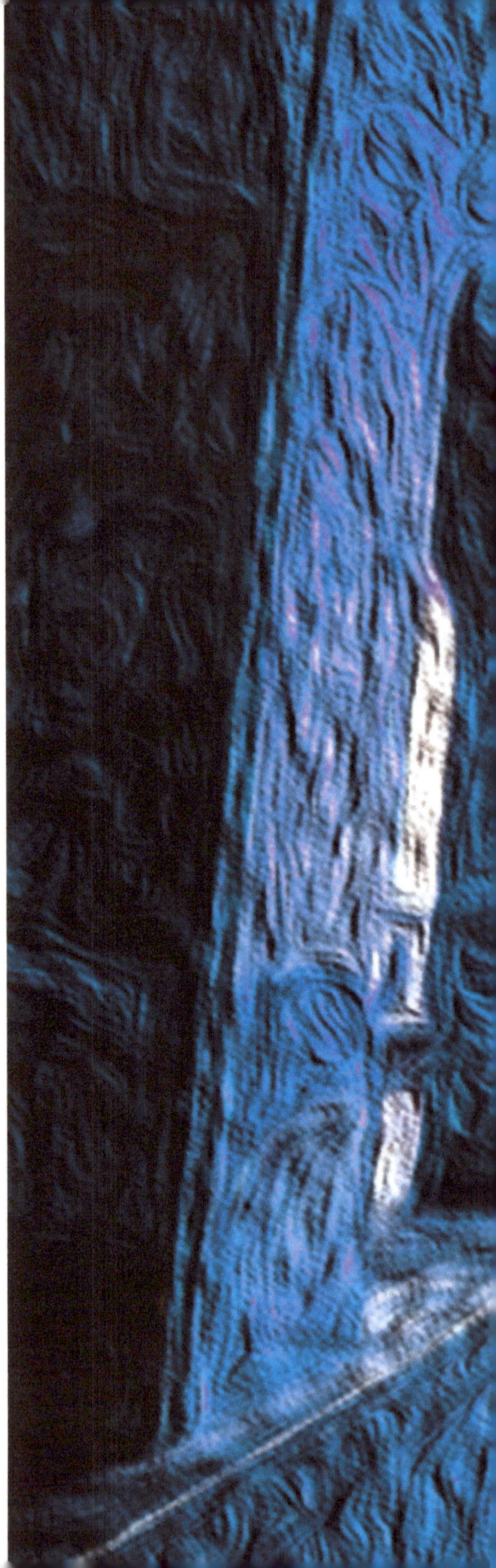

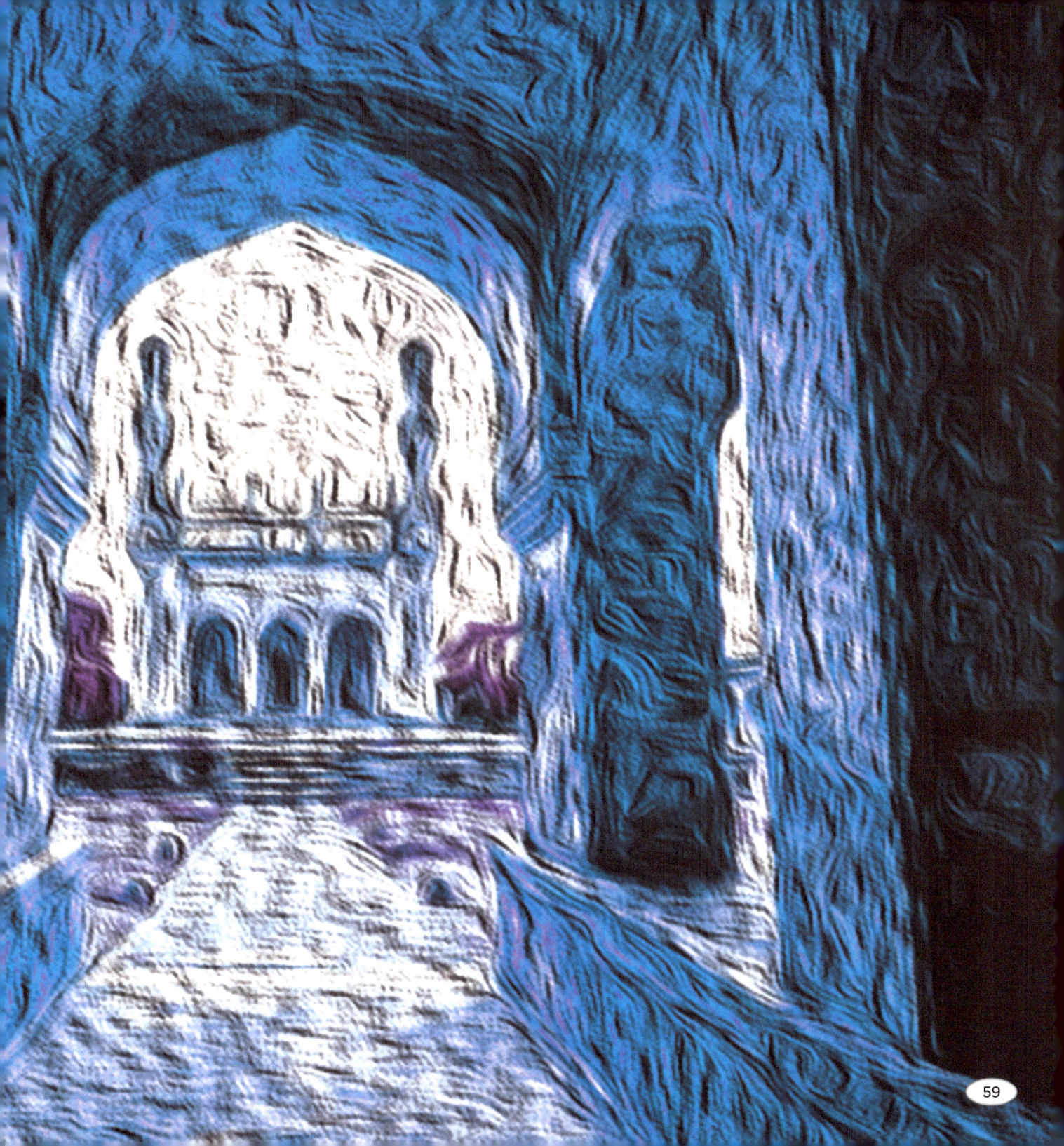

Author Bio

The author is an entrepreneur based in South India with an interest to travel for a long time and to visit natural marvels around the country and the world.

These are his observations on Gandikota in the State of Andhra Pradesh. Gandikota amazed and humbled him. It is a journey of amazement.

Koruvor is the author's pename.

www.ingramcontent.com/pod-product-compliance
Lightning Source LLC
Chambersburg PA
CBHW051048180526
45172CB00002B/555